U.S. Senator Alan Simpson has this to say about THE BEST PART OF AMERICA

Bill Sniffin is a journalist I have come to know well.

He practices his craft with a deft blend of energy, gentleness, devotion and honesty. His work goes beyond the basic journalistic tenets of who, what, when, where, how and why, and instead he seeks to clearly understand and showcase the heart of his community and the people who live there.

His is the kind of journalism that causes people to coalesce, to thoughtfully critique each other and to seek compromise and consensus in a 'little town' within a 'little county' within a 'little state.' His work reflects the heart and soul of an individual who is thoughtful, articulate, incisive and blessed with a deep wellspring of compassion.

Over the years, I remember many an occasion when I have had the opportunity to sit down with Bill and visit about a great assortment of 'stuff.' Each and every time I came away with a better understanding of this fine individual. He works with a kind heart, a marvelously perceptive eye, a wry grin and a love of his fellow humans that is quite singularly evident.

He is a good man who takes a kindly view of the world. He believes in people and that they are here to try to do their very best — and that they most often do. That is why he has been such an important and unique part of the fabric of life of Lander and Fremont County and Wyoming for so many years.

Thank heaven for the Bill Sniffins of the world — working in their own small towns, editing and publishing weekly or bi-weekly papers and continuing to have a positive impact on the lives of their communities.

People like Bill Sniffin — and his kind of journalism — have always been the very Best Part Of America — and they always will be.

THE BEST PART
OF AMERICA

A COLLECTION OF OVER 60 SELECTED STORIES

BY

BILL SNIFFIN

WYOMING'S NATIONAL AWARD-WINNING COLUMNIST

PUBLISHED BY WCS CORPORATION

For information, contact
        WCS Corporation, Publisher,
        P.O. Box 900, Lander, Wyoming 82520

First edition published in 1993 by WCS Corporation.
Book design by Amy Russian.
Illustrations by Eric Sawyer.
Cover photos by Bob Anderson.

ISBN 0-9639350-0-3

For Library of Congress Cataloging in Publication Data, contact the publisher at the address above.

Dedication

This book is dedicated to my wife Nancy
and our children
Alicia, Shelli, Amber and Michael
and their families.

Thanks for being there,
and for making my life a wonderful experience
in THE BEST PART OF AMERICA.

About the Author

by Bill Jones, Wyoming cowboy poet, who was named Wyoming's Funniest Person in 1991.

BILL SNIFFIN IS an unusual sort of guy.

A journalist and newspaper publisher for almost 30 years, Bill is almost the exact opposite of the crusty, cynical, cigarette-puffing newspaper editor common to the breed.

Bill is an optimist in a culture that is dominated by pessimists. He is an upbeat kind of guy in a downbeat world. He believes in the inherent goodness of people, which, to someone in the newspaper business, is a phenomenon that appears all too rarely.

To paraphrase the late comic George Gobel, Bill Sniffin is a pair of brown shoes at a tuxedo affair.

Like an old and comfortable pair of your favorite shoes, *The Best Part of America* is a book that simply makes you feel good.

Like watchin' a young colt frolic in the spring, it is a feeling that is difficult to define. Bill Sniffin's writing is seasoned with humor, compassion and insight. His subjects are things that are vitally important to us all. Family. Wyoming. Friends. The Great American West.

Bill Sniffin is not one to play it safe.

Years ago, he took a chance with a struggling newspaper. He has given a number of aspiring journalists (including me) a shot at making fools of themselves on the printed page — all the way providing encouragement and advice.

In this regard Bill is, I suppose, taking a chance on publishing *The Best Part of America.*

It has no sex, profanity, morbidity, violence, slander, nihilism, anarchy, mayhem, revolutionary politics, kiss-and-tell anecdotes or "touchy-feely" pop psychology.

THERE IS NOT EVEN one chapter telling folks how to get rich in real estate with no money down. It is, however, an unpretentious, varied and highly readable collection of stories that embraces all that is good about living in Wyoming.

Bill Sniffin has his finger on the pulse of small-town America, and I am pleased to report she is alive and doing quite well, thank you.

If you haven't yet met Bill Sniffin, you are, quite frankly, in for a pleasant surprise. Loosen your reins. Take a deep seat, relax and get ready to see some mighty fine country.

Welcome to *The Best Part of America.*

Preface

FOR 23 YEARS, I have been given the distinct privilege of sharing my ideas, experiences and opinions with the people of Wyoming through columns and editorials in the *Wyoming State Journal.*

I consider this to be the greatest experience of my life. People in this state and especially in this valley have treated my family and me with great kindness during this time.

I MOVED TO WYOMING on October 15, 1970. My family joined me a month later. During my first week here when I was "batching it," a friend invited me to the Noble Hotel bar for a drink.

I was the fifth editor at the *Journal* in a two-year period. As I was introduced around, a 6' 6" cowboy reached across the table, grabbed me by my tie, pulled my face right up to his and said:

"I just want to get a good look at you before you're gone."

I somehow find it significant that, of that group of seven guys, I am the only one still in Lander.

THIS BOOK CONTAINS more than 60 of my favorite columns and editorials with several unpublished items thrown in for good measure.

Whenever I find a book that is a collection of articles or stories, I wish the writer would tell me which are his or her favorites. My ten favorites, in no particular order, are:

1) The Best Part Of America
2) Climbing Michael's Mountain
3) The Real Marlboro Man
4) Try to Imagine...
5) Stacy: A story of courage
6) My daughter heads to school
7) A cross at Christmas
8) Give me a morning
9) Evolution of an editor
10) Investigative Reporting #101

WHERE DOES ALL THIS STUFF come from? I have published more than one million words in my career, and the stories in this book are among the best of them.

I want to believe that all of it came directly right out of my head but that is probably not true. These stories come from literally thousands of sources. There are a lot of items published here that I haven't the slightest idea where they came from. I certainly hope there isn't any borrowing of other peoples' work. I have attempted to provide credit where credit is due for other people's work.

The biggest source of material came from the process of just living here in Wyoming for more than two decades. The second biggest came from my family and friends.

THIS 224-PAGE EFFORT has taken a long time to develop. It was fun compiling these stories.

There are people I want to thank for their help in this project. My wife Nancy was there at my side both during the original writing and now during this subsequent effort. Amy Russian served as the graphic artist (and part-time copy editor) who designed the book.

Some typesetting was done by Carla Lebert and much-needed help with the final cuts came from Nancy, our daughter Shelli Johnson, publisher of the *Winner Advocate,* and my sister, Susan Kinneman, an English teacher in Dubois, all very capable copy editors. If any typographical mistakes made it past them, well, so be it!

The final test of a book is whether or not the reader enjoys it. I can only hope that you enjoy reading these items as much as I enjoyed writing them.

— BILL SNIFFIN

P.S. I would love to hear from readers concerning their feelings about what I have written here. Letters can be sent to me at:
P.O. Box 900
Lander, WY 82520
Fax: 307-332-9332

Contents

One

The West

God did so much for Wyoming
that sometimes we think
we don't have to do anything ourselves.

The
Best Part
Of America

Most Americans are friendly
and Wyoming people are the most
friendly of all. And how Americans
always believe in the "American Dream"
— that if they work hard
and don't give up, they will almost
always come out on top.

THE RAIN WAS FALLING IN SHEETS. The wind was howling. And although the temperature was 40 degrees, I could see my breath. My raincoat was soaked through. My umbrella was blown inside out.

It was late at night, and I was standing on a street corner in Cardiff, Wales, waiting for a bus. And I was thinking about the best part of America.

Those Wyoming mountains in my mind were looking pretty good about then.

Wyoming's low humidity and the bright sunshine were only distant memories — but in between shivers, it kept me going.

3

MY VISIT to the Centre for Journalism Studies at the University of Wales was about over. It was almost time to go home. And although it had been a great experience, I couldn't wait to leave.

The Cardiff faculty had invited me to join their mid-career journalism master's program back in the fall of 1986.

The program included journalists from all over the world. There were newspaper editors, television newscasters, magazine editors and government media people.

They came from as far away as the Peoples Republic of China, Malaysia, Korea, Nigeria, Sudan, Ethiopia, Qatar, New Zealand, the United States and other countries, too.

Most of the people in the course were there full-time for two or three years. My master's program was on a part-time basis over three years. While there, my duties also included serving as a guest lecturer to master's candidates from the United Kingdom.

Because of that experience, we have hosted five British reporter interns in subsequent years at our newspaper in Lander.

And the program resulted in a master's degree for me that I finally earned in 1989.

BUT THAT NIGHT IN THE RAIN, all I could think about was my beloved Wyoming.

While I was there, I found that these people wanted to know about America. They liked America, and they liked Americans.

My philosophy has always been to be very polite when I visited another person's country. I never bragged about where I came from and I always complimented them on everything I had found, no matter how hard it was for me to adjust to it.

But once you get beyond the politeness, inevitably the conversation would turn to my part of the country. They wanted to know about this mysterious place called Wyoming.

And I found myself telling them about my part of America. They were fascinated by cowboys and Indians and mountains and Wyoming's famous long distances. I told them about the Oregon Trail and the Pony Express and Yellowstone National Park and Jackson Hole.

I told them about America having 50 states. And Wyoming was just one of those states and that our state has 23 counties. And how Fremont County, my county, was larger than Wales. And despite all that land, only 36,000 people lived there. And how there were nearly 40 places in this county over 13,000 feet in elevation.

I told them about the Grand Teton and Laramie Peak and Devils Tower. I told them about our vast distances and how Wyoming was the least populated state in America with just 400,000 people — about the population of Cardiff.

And I talked about how the wind didn't blow in my hometown of Lander because of our high mountains. And how the sun shone 300 days per year and the humidity was so low, the sky was always blue. And how you couldn't count all the stars in the sky at night. And how easy it was to see more than 100 miles in the distance on a clear day.

ND THEN THERE WAS ALL OUR WILDLIFE plus our wonderful fishing. And I raved about the Red Desert with its wild horses and shifting sand dunes. And South Pass with its gold mines and the firey Red Canyon. And I told them how just a century ago, cavalry and buffalo were roaming these valleys.

Now remember, I believe in being polite when I am in a foreign country. It took a lot to get me to talk about where I came from. But they insisted. They wanted to know more. They just couldn't get enough information about this land I called The Best Part Of America.

I couldn't help smiling when I talked about our clean air and clean water or how wide our streets were. And the great condition of our roads and highways along with all the walking and hiking trails.

Public lands that are available to anybody baffled them. I told them about my spread, the two-million-acre Shoshone National Forest that was just 10 minutes from my home. And how I shared my place with 280 million other Americans.

Then I told them about the Popo Agie River and how it sinks into the ground up there in Sinks Canyon. And the scenic Loop Road with mountain lakes and hiking and camping and mountain climbing. And hot springs and ancient petroglyphs.

And winter activities like snowmobiling, cross country skiing, downhill skiing in Jackson and the State Winter Fair.

And I told them about our diverse population. They were fascinated by my tales of the Shoshone and Arapaho Indians and how well they had preserved their cultures.

5

And I talked about my family. And how most Americans are friendly and Wyoming people are the most friendly of all. And how Americans always believe in the "American Dream" — that if they work hard and don't give up, they will almost always come out on top. I told them how Americans believe the best in people and in situations. How optimism is a national disease in this country.

AND AS I WAS STANDING in the rain that chilly night many years ago, I thought about all these things.

And I realized I lived in The Best Part Of America.

And it was good to know that it was time to go home.

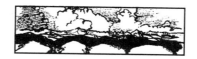

Wyoming's massive mountains

—————⟫•०•⟪—————

These mountains are the landmarks that serve as a lure to cause seemingly intelligent people to alter their present lives and move to Wind River Country to create new lives.

—————⟫•०•⟪—————

THE PIONEERS ALONG THE OREGON TRAIL called the towering Wind River Mountain Range "The Shining Mountains." Most of them had never seen a mountain before, but even if they had, these were different.

The huge granite wall formed by the Winds reflects the morning light to anyone seeing them from a distance. They literally shine.

They are also the highest mountains in Wyoming by quite a bit. I love the Wind River Mountains. When I first saw them in 1970, they made an indelible mark on me that no one can ever take away.

These mountains are the landmarks that serve as a lure to cause seemingly intelligent people to alter their present lives and move to Wind River Country to create new lives. They are doing it by the hundreds, and I don't blame them a bit.

These are truly huge mountains. Following is the main portion of a column I wrote back in the early 1970s about this incredible mountain range and the nearly 40 places in the range higher than 13,000 feet in elevation:

HAVE YOU EVER HEARD of Mt. Turret? Or Mt. Helen?

I hadn't either—yet these two mountains stand 13,620 feet and 13,600 feet tall, two of the very tallest peaks in Wyoming, and they're right out our back door. During our compilation of statistics for *Wind River Country* magazine (a travel guide), we described some of the better-known mountains: Gannett, Fremont, Wind River Peak, Lizard Head, Mt. Hooker and Downs Mountain. Yet, these two peaks are higher than all of those except for Gannett (13,804) and Fremont (13,745).

My source for this information is a fascinating book by Orrin and Lorraine Bonney, well-known mountain experts. The name of the book is *Field Book, Wind River Range.* It contains data on all the mountains of the Wind River Range including climbing routes, hiking trails, and even a chapter of faring in the outdoors. It is a handy little (5x7) book of 200 pages that is designed to fit into a backpack.

Other interesting sites described in this book include the Cirque of Towers, an awe-inspiring place that vaguely resembles a giant crater with a little valley in the middle. A most aptly named lake is located there called Lonesome Lake. The towering, jagged peaks surrounding it are some of the most impressive in the range. Lizard Head, although not the tallest, is the most dramatic. One of the trailheads to get to this place is Dickinson Park.

One of the more interesting areas in our mountain range is a place called "Jackass Pass Trail"—wonder how it got that name? The 10,800-foot pass, which connects Sublette County to Fremont County, allows a traveler to get to the Cirque from the western side. It reportedly got its name from early trappers who claimed that only a jackass could be driven through it.

The book points out there are nearly 40 mountains and peaks in the range that exceed 13,000 feet. Some of the other really towering mountains that are relatively unknown include Mt. Warren (13,720), Jackson Peak (13,517), Doublet Peak (13,600) and Rampart Peak, (13,500).

There is a Mount Lander (12,650) and a place where the wind must really blow: "Howling Wind Pinnacle."

There's a Petzoldt's Pinnacle Ridge, which stands 13,200 feet above sea level (named after famed Lander Mountaineer Paul Petzoldt) along with a place called Gooseneck Pinnacle (some 13,000 feet high).

HERE IS A LIST of some of the other places over 13,000 feet. Read them over and see how many you have heard of:

Ellingwood Peak, Temple Peak, Henderson Peak, Point Mountain, Jackson Peak, Sunset Pinnacle Cathedral Spire, Sunbeam Peak, Horse Ridge, Chimney Rock, Cornice Point.

Also: Mount Febbas, Les Dames Anglaises, Dinwoody Peak, Miriam Peak, Skyline Peak, Bob's Towers, The Sphinx, Mt. Koven, Bastion Peak, Flagstone Peak, Lecestal Peak, Klondike Peak, Bow Mountain, Butchel Peak, Twin Peaks, Mt. Whitecap, Desolation Peak, and Northwest Peak.

There is no other mountain range in the United States like the Wind River Range. The Winds offer experiences to hikers and climbers that will change their lives forever.

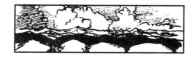

Visit
the desert
—it's beautiful!

A tour of west-central Wyoming's Red Desert in the spring will reveal a world full of life way out of proportion to a desert's normal reputation.

THIS IS NOT THE DESERT you see in the movies.

Picture eagles, deer, antelope, elk, and wild horses frolicking among the green grass, lakes and creeks, aspen trees and flowers—in the desert.

A tour of west-central Wyoming's Red Desert in the spring will reveal a world full of life way out of proportion to a desert's normal reputation.

June is the best time to visit.

Flowers. Would you believe fields of them? Wyoming's state flower, the Indian Paintbrush, flourishes everywhere along with pretty varieties of yellow and blue flowers.

Wildlife was plentiful with all the animals mentioned above. The elk were seen running between Continental Peak and the Oregon Buttes along a line that made up the Continental Divide and separates Fremont County from Sweetwater County.

Rock hunting excursions near the Pickett Lakes and Continental Peak can also be included with guides available from the Bureau of Land Management of where to go and the proper procedures.

Whenever we go, we rarely see a soul besides ourselves throughout the entire day. One year we weren't so fortunate. Some "desert rats" were hunting treasures somewhere out in the middle of the desert, and they were the only other people we saw besides our own group.

I might add we also saw sheepherders, but consider them to be part of the scenery. And a vanishing part of it, too.

Inevitably, when I publish stories about the wonders of the Red Desert, I receive many complaints from veteran rock hounds who know just how interesting the desert is — and they don't want anyone else out there!

I can understand this attitude. It's a great place, equal to the mountains when it comes to outdoor experiences, many people feel, and not nearly as crowded. It is a vast place that too many people scurry through or pass by too fast, thinking it a forbidding area.

According to some sources, the Red Desert is 80 miles by 150 miles in size with reportedly some 4,000 square miles in one unfenced area. This could be the largest unfenced area in the continental United States, and it is vast, to say the least.

As LONG AS A VISITOR stays in the northern part of it, it would be difficult to get lost. Using Crooks and Green Mountain as eastern landmarks, the Wind River Mountains on the north as landmarks, and Continental Peak and the Oregon Buttes as western landmarks, the traveler would be relatively aware of his whereabouts most of the time.

The southern area, though, could be an invitation to disaster without some prominent landmarks to keep in sight.

There are some good roads, although a four-wheel-drive-type vehicle works best but is not necessary.

THE 150TH ANNIVERSARY of the Oregon Trail occurred in 1993, and thousands of people visited the Red Desert for the first time. Most came in late July and August, though, and missed the variety of life that abounds in the desert.

It is a unique place. It's the kind of place that can help a person put the size of the world we live in into some sort of perspective.

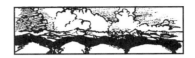

Wyoming isn't empty —it's full

There are even documented cases of tourist buses pulling off the road in between Gillette and Buffalo to take photos of "nothing."

THE VAST PANORAMA OF WYOMING STRETCHED out below me as I flew my airplane over our state one day a few years ago. I was flying from Lander to Rapid City over open country.

It always makes a unique impression to look down and see so much space. Wyoming has such vastness. Critics might call it empty spaces. We locals prefer to call it open spaces.

A recent tourism survey indicated that our vast amounts of open spaces is one of the biggest attractions to people coming here from more populated places. There are even documented cases of tourist buses full of Japanese pulling off the road between Gillette and Buffalo to take photos of "nothing."

So much space with seemingly nothing in it is immensely impressive to the Asian visitor who lives in such crowded conditions. There are also documented cases of those people suffering "reverse claustrophobia" where they actually got ill from the strange feeling of being in a place so open.

A FEW YEARS AGO, there was a national best-selling book that discussed our vastness titled *The Solace of Open Spaces* by Gretel Ehrlich. Some of her comments pulled from the 12 stories in the book include the following:

•The geographic vastness and the social isolation here make emotional evolution seem impossible.

• In all this open space, values crystalize quickly. People are strong on scruples but tenderhearted about quirky behavior.

• If anything is endemic to Wyoming, it is wind. This big room of space is swept out daily, leaving a bone yard of fossils, agates and carcasses in every stage of decay. Though it was water that initially shaped the state, wind is the meticulous gardener, raising dust and pruning the sage.

• The emptiness of the West was for others a geography of possibility.

• The solitude in which Westerners live makes them quiet. They telegraph thoughts and feelings by the way they tilt their heads and listen; pulling their Stetsons into a steep dive over their eyes, or pigeon-toeing one boot over the other, they lean against a fence with a fast wedge of Copenhagen beneath their lower lips and take in the whole scene. These detached looks of quiet amusement are sometimes cynical, but they can also come from a dry-eyed humility as lucid as the air is clear.

• Sagebrush covers 58,000 square miles of Wyoming...despite the desolate look, there's a coziness to living in this state. There are so few people...that ranchers who buy and sell cattle know each other state-wide.

• To live and work in this kind of open country, with its hundred-mile views, is to lose the distinction between background and foreground. When I asked an older ranch hand to describe Wyoming's openness, he said, "it's all a bunch of nothing — wind and rattlesnakes — and so much of it, you can't tell where you're going or where you've been and it doesn't make much difference."

Ms. Ehrlich's comments are beautifully written, and I'd strongly recommend people buy her book.

FROM MY VANTAGE POINT in that airplane, Wyoming didn't look empty. It looked like a kaleidoscope of colors, as river-formed valleys, mountains and hills jutted and swirled along. Patches of snow would indicate how fast or how recently the wind had been blowing across the desert.

Wyoming isn't empty. It's full. It is just a matter of knowing what you are looking at...and looking for.

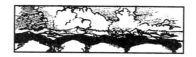

Advocating abandoning the Great Plains

Telecommunications and computers will
conquer the enemies of
Plains progress and prosperity —
distance, isolation, income dependent
on the whims of weather and wells —
by making geography irrelevant.

FIRST IT WAS A WHISPER. Then a murmur. Now this new idea is mentioned often in major publications as if the idea were sound. And people of the West should be listening.

The ideas of Frank and Deborah Popper of Rutgers University (New Jersey) are being accepted as gospel by many people all across America, especially those living in the more populated regions.

Called "Buffalo Commons," their plan is to take much of the land out here in the Great Plains of the West and turn it back to the Buffalo.

They refer to this part of the country as that area west of the 98th meridian, which runs through eastern North and South Dakota, Nebraska, Kansas and Oklahoma.

This vast area is the size of Western Europe. It contains nearly a sixth of the land in the USA but only two percent of the country's population lives here. It contains a place I call The Best Part Of America, too.

AN ARTICLE in the May, 1993 edition of *Outside* Magazine spent 10 pages on the subject.

They quote the Poppers' statistics where they claim this part of the country has been abused and overgrazed, and that populations are leaving in droves.

"We are not trying to depopulate Denver or Dallas," Frank Popper says in the article. "Cities and healthy towns lie well away from the distressed areas affected by the Buffalo Commons. We're talking free-market, gradual, generations-long change."

IN THE SAME ARTICLE, Phil Burgess of the Center for the New West in Denver sees an opposite situation.

He is cited as pointing out that great progress will occur in this part of the country in the next century. "Telecommunications and computers will at last conquer the traditional enemies of Plains progress and prosperity — distance, isolation, income dependent on the whims of weather and wells — by making geography irrelevant."

Both the views of the Poppers and the views of regional leaders like Burgess are important to people who live in the West.

AS WESTERNERS, people here often find their voices are muted when it comes to controlling national opinion.

A radical idea like that being promoted by the Poppers isn't unusual. The people of this part of the country are used to being dominated by the larger population of people who live outside this area and want to dictate its future.

It would be wise for people who love this part of America to stay tuned to this discussion and be prepared to defend your western lifestyle with every bit of strength you have.

I think the arguments posed by Burgess are among the best ever stated about the West. He is a true leader of Western America and is someone everybody in the region should be listening to.

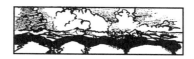

Great Buffalo Herd Monument

The honor or blame for the idea
of this giant drawing in the desert
lies with this writer.

WHEN NEARLY 100 PEOPLE turned out on Beaver Rim 30 miles southeast of Lander in August of 1993 to view a huge drawing of a buffalo, it marked the true beginning of a project known as the Great Buffalo Herd Monument.

This project was first hatched locally two years ago when a buffalo rancher on Long Island, New York called Lander buffalo rancher Dave Raynolds about artist Bob Berks' dream of a monument to the vast herds that once roamed the United States.

Berks' project involves a herd of 1,000 sculpted copper buffalo.

However, the story of how one of the largest drawings in the world came into being has a different (and local) twist.

The honor or blame for the idea of this giant drawing in the desert lies with this writer.

HAVING GROWN UP in northeast Iowa, I was always fascinated by earth art. The ancient Indian tribes there created the Effigy Mounds,

17

which is a now a national monument. The artwork created by these Indians featured superb drawings of animals that meant a lot to them, like bear, deer, snakes and birds. I brought that fascination with earth art to this project.

Raynolds got me involved with Berks and the buffalo project two years ago. As a member of the Wyoming Travel Commission, I had seen statistics that showed that central Wyoming was continuing to lose its tourism market share. This part of the state could use an attraction besides the Oregon Trail, South Pass City, the Wind River Mountains and the Wind River Indian Reservation. It seemed logical that a monument to the buffalo could be a good idea, especially when you consider that herds of 60,000 buffalo used to roam the Beaver Rim area.

One morning at the Maverick Restaurant in Lander, I was having breakfast with Berks and his wife Tod. I told them I was having a problem with how his idea of 1,000 copper buffalos would look. Would they just be scattered over a vast area? Would they be clumped together?

As a pilot, I had flown over the various sites being considered for the monument and in looking at the maps, I noticed that the sites were smack in the center of Wyoming.

Wyoming is shaped in a square and the buffalo is the state's symbol, located in the middle of the square state flag.

"Why not create a large drawing of a buffalo there in the desert that would provide a focus for the entire herd?" I suggested to Berks. I drew it out on the back of a place mat.

Berks greeted the idea enthusiastically. He had wanted to create a monument that you could see from a distance (to appreciate the herd size), up close (to appreciate the individual size of the buffalo), individual sculptures that would move in the wind (to make them life-like) and to even add sound, through the use of special wind devices (to give people a feeling about a buffalo herd that they could never get from live buffalo, because live buffalo can be quite dangerous.)

In a gesture of optimism, Berks and I both signed and dated that place mat with a laugh and it's stored safely in my files.

AND I MUST SAY, it was a thrill that August evening to stand on the bluff overlooking that drawing and to see the manifestation of an idea that was hatched on a place mat that long ago.

Berks, with the help of local engineer Charlie Spurlock, had created a beautiful drawing of a buffalo in the desert. It is located in an area interspersed with lots of jeep trails and yet the lines of Berks' drawing meshed beautifully with the curves of the surrounding bluffs.

The view took me back to my childhood when our family would troop among those ancient Indian designs, which were drawn in tribute to the animals that meant so much to all of them.

And today, we are treated to a modern-day rendition of such a work of earthen art.

THE ARTWORK WAS A CENTERPIECE of an eight-minute segment of the CBS-TV *Sunday Morning Show* with Charles Kuralt shown in September, 1993.

A photo of the huge drawing was snapped by photographers for *National Geographic* and is scheduled to run in an issue of the 10-million-edition magazine soon.

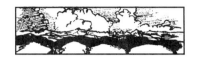

Home On The Range

Home, home on the Range.
Where the deer and the antelope play.

ABOUT THE ONLY THINGS that I thought were unique about the song "Home on the Range" were that it reminded me of Wyoming, and that it could have been the theme song both for our long-time correspondent from the Sweetwater area, Beulah Peterson, and for local buffalo rancher Dave Raynolds.

Back in 1988, those ideas changed when actor Wilford Brimley approached the microphone during his speech at the One Shot Antelope Hunt banquet that year. Without much fanfare, the grizzled movie veteran stepped up to the front of the audience.

The crowd readied itself for some sage advice or wicked humor. But not so. Brimley, who is a real ex-rancher, had talked sincerely throughout his weekend in Lander of his earlier lives as an unsuccessful sheep rancher in Idaho. He had known hardship, and he appreciated the good life he was enjoying now. He had been emotionally moved by his experience in Lander and the Wind River Mountains and the vast Red Desert.

It prompted him to recite some words that moved the audience immensely.

BRIMLEY RECITED four lesser known verses of the song "Home on the Range" as a poem. Those verses were as follows:

20

How often at night when the heavens are bright
with the light from the glittering stars,
have I stood there amazed and asked as I gazed if their glory exceeds that of ours.

Oh, I love these wild flowers in this dear land of ours,
the curlew I love to hear scream,
and I love the white rocks and the antelope flocks that graze on the mountain-tops
green.

Oh, give me a land where the bright diamond sand
flows leisurely down to the stream,
where a graceful white swan goes gliding along like a maid in a heavenly dream.

Then I would not exchange my home on the range,
where the deer and the antelope play;
where seldom is heard a discouraging word and the skies are not cloudy all day.

THE CROWD was moved, too, as he recited those stanzas from memory.

It caused me to wonder just where the song came from originally. The staff of the Lander library, Roberta Olson, Alex Tipton and Doris Geer, researched the song and came up with the verses and some history.

The song was popularized in the 1920s by a Texan named David Guion, who also wrote songs such as "Carry Me Back to the Lone Prairie" and "The Yellow Rose of Texas."

The original words, though, have been claimed to be written by two people, Dr. Brewster Higley of Beaver Creek, Kansas and Dan Kelly, his neighbor, back in the 1870s. It's been called the "Cowboy's National Anthem." But few people ever get past the first verse.

Those other verses, by the way, are as follows:

Where the air is so pure, the zephyrs so free,
the breezes so balmy and light,
that I would not exchange my home on the range for all the cities so bright.

The red man was pressed from his part of the West,
he's likely no more to return
to the banks of Red River where seldom if ever their flickering camp fires burn.

Rising From The Plains

McPhee writes in a style that vividly lets you imagine the extreme risings of mountain ranges, the descent of valleys and the rolling together of various land masses.

I T'S BEEN SAID THERE ARE NO BORING STORIES, just boring writers. And with that thought it mind, it would seem that a book about geology would be interesting only to geologists.

The book *Rising From The Plains* by author John McPhee ranks as one of the most interesting and most important books ever written about Wyoming.

McPhee uses the life of famed geologist David Love as the centerpiece of this book. Love grew up in Fremont County and graduated from high school in Lander. He has long been considered the dean of geologists in the Rocky Mountain region.

M CPHEE CAPTURES THE WESTERN SPIRIT of Love's life and that of his parents as they carved out a unique existence on a ranch in an area of Fremont County near Castle Gardens.

The book is full of references to Lander, Fremont County and the unique geology of Wyoming. McPhee writes in a style that vividly lets you imagine the extreme risings of mountain ranges, the descent of valleys and the rolling together of various land masses.

Intertwined with the geological stories (told mostly through Love's words) is the life story of the famous geologist and his mother, who came west in 1905 after graduating Phi Beta Kappa from Wellesley College back east.

The book was serialized in three parts in the *New Yorker Magazine* a few years ago.

IN ONE PART, McPhee writes about Love attending school in Lander (he and his brother were educated at home by their mother until they were ready for high school):

"Their mother rented a house in Lander and stayed there with them while they attended Fremont County Vocational High School. One of their classmates was William Shakespeare, whose other name was War Bonnet. Lander at that time was the remotest town in Wyoming. It advertised itself as 'the end of the rails and the start of the trails.'"

The Love Ranch was one of those outposts that was so far from everything else that anyone passing through would stop. Often, people would sleep in the bunkhouse and join the Loves for dinner.

MCPHEE WRITES about one memorable meal:

"People like that came along with such frequency that David's mother eventually assembled a chronicle called 'Murderers I Have Known.' She did not publish the manuscript or even give it much private circulation, in her regard for the sensitivities of some of the first families of Wyoming. As David would one day comment, 'they were nice men, family friends, who had put away people who needed killing, and she did not wish to offend them — so many of them were such decent people.'

"One of these was Bill Grace. Homesteader and cowboy, he was one of the most celebrated murderers in central Wyoming, and he had served time, but people generally disagreed with the judiciary and felt that Bill, in the acts for which he was convicted, had only been 'doing his civic duty.'

"At the height of his fame, he stopped at the ranch one afternoon and stayed for dinner. Although David and (his brother) Allen were young boys, they knew exactly who he was, and in his presence were struck dumb with awe.

"As it happened, they had come upon and dispatched a rattle-snake that day — a big one, over five feet long. Their mother decided to serve it creamed on toast for dinner. She and their father sternly instructed David and Allen not to use the word 'rattlesnake' at the table. They were to refer to it as chicken, since a possibility existed that Bill Grace might not be an eater of adequate sophistication to enjoy the truth.

"The excitement was too much for the boys. Despite the parental injunction, gradually their conversation at the table fished its way toward the snake. Casually — while the meal was going down — the boys raised the subject of poisonous vipers, gave their estimates of the contents of local dens, told stories of snake encounters, and so forth. Finally, one of them remarked on how very good rattlers were to eat.

"Bill Grace said, 'By God, if anybody ever gave me rattlesnake meat, I'd kill them.'

"The boys went into a state of catatonic paralysis. In the pure silence, their mother said, 'More chicken, Bill?'

"'Don't mind if I do,' said Bill Grace."

AND THOSE STORIES are just a few that are included in this wonderful book. It is must reading for people who are interested in a well-written story about Wyoming's recent past and long-distant past.

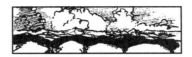

Looped

We were tired and dusty.
But we were again renewed
by the spirit that getting "looped"
can do for a person.

THERE WE WERE — stuffed from a picnic lunch — relaxing in the sun while a soft breeze rustled through the trees at Louis Lake, above Lander on the Loop Road.

It's a scene repeated over and over by local people each summer. The popular lake is surrounded by wonderful picnicking areas. The fishing is good, too, as anglers from boats and the beach would testify.

We were on a family outing that is so typical for us and similar to scores of other trips. Our family loves this trip.

THIS PARTICULAR SUNDAY dawned as one of the beautiful Wyoming summer days. You could tell it was the second official day of summer. For a change, no mid-afternoon thunderstorm reared up to dampen spirits.

We headed out of Lander and up through Red Canyon. The flowers were beyond belief. They started out a brilliant purple, then turned to red and then turned to yellow. The entire hillside on Red Canyon was a sea of yellow flowers.

The flowers and the green grass against the red canyon walls made for a colorful setting more suitable for a painting than a photograph.

South Pass City was booming on that Sunday, with the parking lot nearly full. The new road entering into the old ghost town appeared to be working quite well.

WE THEN TOOK THE LOOP ROAD south out of the town which circled around back to Highway 28. That took us along the Oregon Trail which was the subject of a six-state celebration in 1993 as the trail celebrated its 150th anniversary.

Lander native Randy Wagner headed Wyoming's version of that celebration. Nobody could have done that job better. Wagner's famous movie *The First Road West* is still the best documentary we've ever seen on the subject.

WE THEN HEADED DOWN the Loop Road from the South Pass end and encountered that rough washboard about three miles in. The roadbed looks in great shape there, except for occasional washboarding. Cars that slow down will do fine, but a motorist driving over 25 miles per hour in some places there could shake the wax out of his or her ears.

Louis Lake was a jewel but it was disappointing to see that Louis Lake Lodge wasn't open. That great old facility is the subject of an ongoing U.S. Forest Service review. Let's hope that somehow the lodge gets opened and perhaps expanded. It is too bad that such a wonderful facility, with such a great potential, is shuttered during the busy summer season. Just think of the potential for that facility during snowmobile season.

As we passed Blue Ridge at the 9,600 feet elevation sign, we recalled the wonderful picnics our family had enjoyed at the Blue Ridge lookout. It is one of the most unique places on the Loop Road. The old lookout was built during the Depression, I believe, and served as a place to watch for forest fires. The view from up there is spectacular in all directions

ON OUR WAY BACK TO LANDER, we stopped for awhile to admire the size of Frye Lake Reservoir. It was huge. The large amount of rain and melted snowpack could be seen in the expanded size of this lake.

On our way down the switchbacks, we stopped to take more photos of the sea of yellow flowers on the hillside. The flowers were in their final stages of display.

At the entrance to Sinks Canyon State Park, two mountain climbers were near the top of that rock wall. They were enjoying their perilous perch as we stopped and snapped a few photos.

Then we headed home. Our six-hour trip was over. We were tired and dusty. But we were again renewed by the spirit that getting "looped" can do for a person.

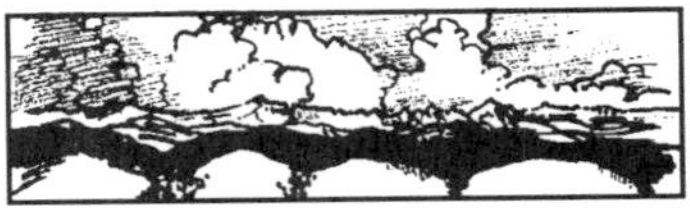

Our Indian neighbors

After having attended many Sun Dances, both Shoshone and Arapaho, I can say that it is impossible for someone to attend one of these and to walk away the same.

ONE OF THE MOST UNIQUE and rewarding aspects of spending two decades in west-central Wyoming has been the exposure to the cultures of the Shoshone and Arapaho Indian tribes.

Nowhere in Wyoming can a culture claim a history more than a couple of centuries old. Yet here are two tribal cultures that extend back thousands of years. Following are some snapshots out of my memory banks of some Indian experiences:

LONG BEFORE ANY WHITE MAN ever knew the vast beauty of what was to become Wyoming, the land was the favorite place of numerous Indian tribes.

Those early peoples loved this country just like we all love it today. These vast spaces also provided them with protection from their enemies and provided the grazing for tens of thousands of buffalo.

Theirs was often a hunting culture. The Indians were environmentally conscious before such an idea became a trend. They used everything and they recycled.

Favorite sites among those early Shoshone Indians were the warm valleys in the Fort Washakie area and especially the hot springs there and at Thermopolis. They went on hunting expeditions into the Wind River Mountains and evidence showed they had many hunting camps on South Pass between present-day Lander and Rock Springs.

WHO COULD EVER FORGET the first time they attended an Indian Sun Dance?

For this ceremony is not really a dance in the white man's conventional experience, but rather an intense, deeply moving religious experience.

After having attended many Sun Dances, both Shoshone and Arapaho, I can say that it is impossible for someone to attend one of these and to walk away the same.

Young men of the tribe dance in the hopes that their prayers for family or friends are answered. Or for thanksgiving for some good event that has occurred to them. The ceremony is sober and somber.

I don't claim to know a lot about the ceremony, but it involves intense fasting by the dancer and the strongest physical commitment. I feel privileged that Indians allow white people to come and watch, as I do, in respectful awe.

THEN THERE ARE THE POWWOWS. These are great community events — the Indian equivalent of a county fair. Non-Indians are welcomed and can even dance once in a while, when they have the community round dance.

Food is aplenty. I seem to share the tastes of the Powwow crowd — "Give me another Indian Taco, will ya?"

"OUR HOPE IS WITH our young people," the middle-aged Indian leader was saying. "And despite an occasional setback, I believe we are succeeding."

Former Chairman of the Shoshone Tribal Council, John Washakie, couldn't help but be optimistic. Washakie is a handsome 50-year old man, with coal black hair and bright eyes. He chooses his words carefully, and is very articulate, especially as a man who has testified a dozen times before Congressional committees.

The former long-time tribal chairman is a distant grandson of the great Chief Washakie, the famous leader of the Shoshone Tribe.

Washakie is joined by other leaders in seeking a better life for young people on the reservation.

The current crop of leaders, who are mostly Washakie's age, represent a major shift in power on the Wind River Indian Reservation.

Shoshones like Darwin St. Clair, Floyd Phillips, Richard Burnett, West Martel and Don Aragon and many others represent this new generation of leaders. Arapahos like Harvey Spoonhunter, Pat and Rupert Goggles and Richard Ortiz and many others are also showing great leadership qualities.

Other Indian leaders like Dick Baldes have provided great examples through agencies like the U.S. Fish and Wildlife Service, which Baldes heads.

We publish a community newspaper on the reservation called the *Wind River News,* which we have done for 11 years. During this time, we have been fortunate to have met so many of these bright, ambitious young people who are really going places. And with the help of their elders, these young men and women have a good grip on the future of their tribes.

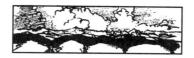

Oregon Trail: The First Road West

The Oregon Trail was a natural travel
route over the prairies and the Rocky
Mountains. It was a general route West
with almost as many branches,
diversions, cutoffs and shortcuts
as there were wagon masters.

VISITORS CAN FOLLOW THE FIRST ROAD WEST as it travels through
western Wyoming.

Travelers on the famous Oregon Trail can follow in the footsteps
of pioneers, mountain men, Pony Express riders, cowboys and
Indians by following the historic trail through Wyoming.

Considered the route of the largest voluntary mass migration of
people in human history, this road served 350,000 people during a
27-year period 150 years ago.

The trail spans the width of Wyoming. Visitors to west-central
Wyoming can relive those experiences endured by their ancestors in
making this historic march from 1841 to 1868.

The 150th anniversary of the Oregon Trail was celebrated throughout Wyoming during the summer of 1993.

THE TRAIL IS AN EASY DRIVE FROM LANDER, Riverton or Casper and makes for an excellent loop drive.

The logical starting place would be Independence Rock near the junction of highways 287 and 220, 88 miles east of Lander on a good paved federal highway.

The famous Independence Rock, with all its carvings of names and dates, is a good starting point, using Lander as a base. Travelers may take Highway 287 to the rock, and then come back to Devil's Gate and turn off and visit the Tom Sun Ranch. This is on the original trail and the ruts are visible. On a nearby sagebrush covered hill are many pioneer graves, originally covered with rocks to protect them from coyotes.

Markers tell of Martin's Cove and other historic spots. From Independence Rock, the Oregon Trail followed the Sweetwater River to South Pass, near the headwaters of the river. Split Rock is visible for miles and the Old Castle can be seen from the highway.

The highway crossed Ice Slough, a long, narrow, boggy stream winding through a semi-desert waste. During winters the waters froze to great depths and pioneer diaries tell how they dug up ice even in mid-summer.

At the site of St. Mary's Station, also called Rocky Ridge Station, the trail left the banks of the Sweetwater and ran several miles to the north of the river. A car cannot travel much of the trail unless the traveler is driving a four-wheel-drive vehicle.

From Lander take Highway 287 to the junction of 28 and 287 and stay on Highway 28. This takes the traveler to South Pass and past Sweetwater bridge there are a number of road markers. You are right on the trail here and can go either right or left on it. A four-wheel-drive vehicle is needed and visitors should take someone along who knows the country. They can take those interested to the "Parting of the Ways" where California-bound wagons left the Oregon Trail.

The highway has many marked historic sites along the way and information is available at South Pass City and Atlantic City.

THE OREGON TRAIL accounts for much of the history a visitor will encounter in his travels through central Wyoming, and as you travel through this section of Big Wyoming, you will encounter markers, historic sites, museums, wagon ruts, military establishments, trading posts and stagecoach and Pony Express stations, all of which owe their existence to "The First Road West."

The Oregon Trail was a natural travel route over the prairies and the Rocky Mountains. It was a general route West with almost as many branches, diversions, cutoffs and shortcuts as there were wagon masters. The trail existed because of the North Platte and Sweetwater rivers, and the gradual, natural grade offered to cross the "Shining Mountains" at South Pass. Its outer limits of the trail were tied only to the width of these river valleys.

The significance of the stretch from Fort Laramie in eastern Wyoming (Goshen County) to South Pass in central Wyoming (Fremont County) is that all the major emigrant trails came together to follow the same route. There are a number of trails leading into Fort Laramie and a number branch off from South Pass, but in this 250-mile stretch across Wyoming, everyone "Went Westering" together.

THE MOUNTAIN MAN — that colorful character born of the fur trade who has intrigued so many historians — is credited with pioneering the trail across Wyoming. He had been in the Rockies, off and on, more than three decades prior to the commencement of the momentous overland emigration in 1841.

During the 27-year period of mass overland emigration by covered wagon that began in 1841, the mountain man's pathway along the North Platte and Sweetwater rivers to South Pass would be known by almost as many names as there were pioneer parties following it.

The California Road was the name preferred by the thousands of Forty-Niners, the gold seekers, who rushed along its length in search of the "Mother Lode" between 1849-52. The same route was known as the Mormon Trail by the thousands of faithful who followed Brigham Young away from a place of religious persecution in Illinois and into the new freedom of the Salt Lake Valley from 1847 to 1856.

For a brief period during 1860-61, the exciting Pony Express made use of the route to carry the mail between Sacramento and St. Joseph, Mo. in an unbelievably quick nine days, and the Pony Express Route became a real name for the historic old trail.

Others called it simply the Emigrant Road or the Overland Road, for indeed it was. Geographic names, such as the Great Platte River Road and the South Pass Highway found some favor.

THE OREGON TRAIL is the name that was most used, that is the most appropriate and that has survived the test of history. (The word "trail" satisfies the modern concept of the route. Pioneers who used it always called it a "road" and, from their frame of reference, it was.)

The name Oregon Trail does no honor to the present state of Oregon, for no such state existed in pioneer days. Rather, it called attention to the trail's overall destination in a vast, uncharted wilderness of land in the Pacific Northwest known loosely as "Oregon Country."

Pioneers entered this "Oregon Country" by crossing the Continental Divide at South Pass, located in the southwest corner of present-day Fremont County. "Today we have entered Oregon," wrote one pioneer on crossing the pass. "We nooned beyond at a small spring and drank the waters of the Pacific!"

A chain of high hills just west of South Pass was named "The Oregon Buttes" by pioneers.

South Pass, then, became the key that unlocked the northwest for the United States — there was no other natural pass through the rugged chain of the Rocky Mountains that could be negotiated by covered wagon traffic. The mountain men and pioneers chose the route so well that it remains as a major traffic route through central Wyoming today.

TO FOLLOW THE GENERAL ROUTE of the Oregon Trail on modern, blacktop highways, take U.S. 26 between Torrington and Casper; Wyo. 220 between Casper and Muddy Gap Junction; U.S. 287 between Muddy Gap Junction and Lander; and Wyo. 28 southwest to South Pass. By following all, or any part, of this route, you will be seeing Wyoming's landmarks and historic sites much as they were first seen by the people who opened the West.

Wyoming is just about the only state that has miles of the original Oregon Trail visible and even traversable. Elsewhere time and progress has taken its toll on the most historic trail in the West.

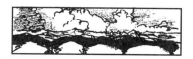

Introducing Europeans to Wyoming

The answer is "Yes, we do know how
lucky we are to live in this place."
And we want to share it
with our European friends. We know
that you will love this place, too.

*(Note: Following is a talk that I gave to a group of European travel
agents who were visiting Wyoming through a company that I co-founded
called Rocky Mountain International. That company does international
marketing for the states of Wyoming, South Dakota, Idaho and Montana.)*

ON BEHALF OF ROCKY MOUNTAIN INTERNATIONAL, I want to welcome
you to the Great American Rocky Mountains.

My partner, Chuck Box, and I are pleased that you could make
this familiarization trip. You are in for a special treat today when you
visit the world's first national park — Yellowstone.

I spent quite a bit of time in your part of the world between 1986
and 1988. I earned a Masters Degree at the University of Wales in
Great Britain. While over there, I made several trips to the Continent.

You come from a very beautiful part of the world. I loved the flowers, the windmills, the canals and the trains. And the people were very, very friendly. I compliment you on your people and your country.

Yours is a somewhat flatter world compared to our part of the world wouldn't you say? And you have a little more water and our country is a little more brown than yours, which is very colorful.

Today you will visit that jewel of the Rocky Mountains — Yellowstone National Park.

Recently, I gave a tour of Yellowstone to a Luxembourg-based journalist named Adrien Weber. He turned to me at one point and said "Do you realize how lucky you are to live in this place?"

The answer was "Yes, we do know how lucky we are to live in this place." And we want to share it with our European friends. We know that they will love this place, too.

While I had his attention, I told him about an unusual experience I had had with an Irish tourist that summer. That was also the topic of a column that I wrote for the *Journal*. It is reprinted below:

An Irishman finds the Oregon Trail

Have you ever thought how the Rocky Mountain West must look like to a foreign traveler?

Last spring, I was stopped along the highway about 25 miles north of Lander when a rental car pulled up across the road from me. I was using a portable phone calling my office and had to stop because road was about to drop down into a canyon.

Pretty soon, someone was thumping my window.

With a start, I put down my phone, cautiously looked around and found this middle-aged man (about my age) looking through the window at me. He motioned me to roll down the window.

He said his name was Ed Tuthill and he was looking for the Oregon Trail. He and his son were visiting the Rocky Mountain region by rental car and he couldn't quite figure out where the trail was.

They had visited Mount Rushmore, the Bighorn Battlefield, Glacier Park, Yellowstone and other sights. They were now headed to the Oregon Trail. Well, he was about 80 miles north of it, which I explained to him and then gave him a couple of copies of the *Wind*

River Country travel guide that I had in my car. So, off they went, headed south.

THE STORY DOESN'T END THERE. A letter arrived several months later from Ed and his son thanking me for the directions and for the copies of Wind River Country.

He wrote: "...growing up in the fifties and goin' to the pictures once or maybe twice a week and every other film being a western, names like 'Wyoming' and the 'Oregon Trail' were commonplace.

"I must confess I thought the trail just did not exist any more, that it had been ploughed under or built on. Indeed, I felt much the same about the West in general.

"A few years ago, I borrowed some books from the library and a picture of the West began to form in my mind of a vast country, much of it unspoilt. The prairies, the mountains and, of course, the Oregon Trail.

"My son and I started to save for what we called the holiday of a lifetime and that's what it turned out to be. We were away for five weeks and travelled through 12 states and covered 8,000 miles.

"I want to thank you again for the *Wind River Country,* and if I ever get the opportunity to travel to the west again, I'll call and say hello!"

"All the best,"
Edward Tuthill, Green Briar, Laughanure Clane
Co. Kildare, Ireland.

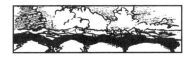

Jackson Hole: Home of big rocks and rockin' nightlife

The people of Jackson are among the
friendliest in the country
and they offer big-town hospitality
in a small-town atmosphere.

THE MOST SPECTACULAR MOUNTAINS in the world greet the visitor to
Jackson Hole, Wyoming. This valley is the home of the fabulous
Tetons and Grand Teton National Park.

The mountains are among the youngest in the country at nine
million years old, according to geologists. This is 40 million years
younger than other mountains in this part of Wyoming.

The early French trappers who discovered these mountains
thought they resembled breasts and thus named them "the Tetons."

The Grand Teton is the second highest mountain in Wyoming at
13,766 feet above sea level. Only Gannett Peak in Fremont County
is higher at 13,804.

THAT DESCRIBES THE ROCKS in Jackson Hole, but what about the rockin'?

On that score, the town of Jackson is the liveliest town in Wyoming during the summer and winter.

This rockin' little town boasts more than 100 restaurants, many of them world-class. Motels and hotels abound, as do guest ranches and bed and breakfast facilities.

As you drive into Jackson from the north, on your left is the Wyoming Visitor Information Center. The local Chamber of Commerce also is located there, and the friendly staff will help you find your way around.

The list of "what to do" is almost endless. It ranges from rides on ski lifts and alpine slides to tram rides, river rafting, lake trips, fishing, hiking, horseback riding, eating, drinking, dancing, partying, sightseeing, camping, watching wildlife, museums and art gallery hopping and more.

The wildlife in all of Wyoming is unsurpassed in the continental United States. Jackson Hole is no exception. The sharp-eyed tourist may even spot a bald eagle. Watch for moose which roam at will throughout the valley along with occasional black bears, elk and deer.

Visitors to the Grand Teton National Park can view special displays in the visitor centers. There are more than 200 miles of trails in the park along with a series of spectacular lakes including vast Jackson Lake.

Jackson Hole is the playground of Wyoming. Local Wyoming citizens tend to spend 10 months a year going to Jackson, but stay away in July and August because of the crowds of tourists.

I HAD THE GOOD FORTUNE to serve Teton County as its representative on the Wyoming Travel Commission for four years (1989-93) and also served on the Jackson Hole Visitors Council during that time.

I served on that Visitor Council with Clay James, Manuel Lopez, Mark Rohde, Joe Byron, Helen Kudar and Tom Robbins, plus it gave me the chance to work with such outstanding citizens as Clarene Law, Suzanne Young, Mark Weakland, Joe Rogers, Carol Waller, Pam and Jerry Rankin, Sara Flitner, Dick Scarlett, Bob Lalonde, Ed and Lee Riddell and many others whom I'm afraid I've left out.

Our family loves to ski at Jackson Hole Ski Area which is ably represented by Harry Baxter and Kari Gemmel. That mountain is undergoing a tremendous upgrade under its new owners, the Resors and the Kemmerers, which will be wonderful for local and non-local skiers, alike.

█ T'S ESTIMATED that more than three million people a year visit the incredibly scenic Jackson Hole. And to Wyomingites, who tend to crave space, the crowds that descend during the last two months of summer often transform this gorgeous valley to a jam that looks like southern California when it comes to traffic.

But even if that is the only time a person can go to Jackson Hole, it's well worth it. The people of Jackson are among the friendliest in the country, and they offer big-town hospitality with a small-town atmosphere.

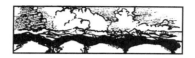

Colorado Rockies games had a Wyoming flavor

Baseball is my favorite sport
and the chance to be at those first two
games will rank up there
as among my favorite thrills.

(Note: The Colorado Rockies finished their first season with an incredible record of 67-95. They set an all-time major league attendance record. It was a wonderful season for everyone in the Mountain Time Zone. The article below was written after the Rockies' first two games in Denver.)

DENVER — How sweet could it be?

Sweet, very sweet.

I was fortunate enough to be in the press box and along the playing field when the Colorado Rockies played their first two home baseball games in history. And they won them both convincingly.

The games had a big Wyoming connection.

• Governor Mike Sullivan helped Colorado Governor Roy Romer throw out the first ball in the second game Saturday.

41

• U. S. Senator Al Simpson was on hand with former Colorado Senator Tim Wirth at Friday's opener, having helped Wirth with a Senate push that pressured the National League into making expansion baseball possible.

• On Saturday, Wyoming was saluted as the first state in the region to have supported the arrival of big league baseball.

• Montreal was led during the three-game series by former Casper star Mike Lansing. Lansing also was the first player to ever have a big league at bat at Mile High Stadium in this first season.

THE GAMES WERE A DREAM come true for me. Baseball is my favorite sport and the chance to be at those first two games will rank up there among my favorite thrills.

There were 700 members of the press at Mile High Stadium gathered for the historic time. At times, the overall noise of the press box sounded like popcorn popping with all the portable computer keyboards being pounded on by the writers in attendance.

Just being there was the high point.

Who could soon forget Eric Young hitting a home run on a 3-2 pitch in the first at-home at-bat by a Rockie?

The rest of the game just got better as the Rockies rolled to an 11-1 lead. I was one of the few people there not disappointed when Lansing hit a three-run home run with two outs in the ninth inning. The game wrapped at 11-4. History had been made. There were 80,227 people present. It was the largest crowd in history in the entire Major Leagues. It was the first real major league game ever played in the Mountain Time Zone.

The three-day home stand also set a new all-time record with more than 200,000 people attending. This broke a record that had stood since 1948 when the Yankees played at Cleveland. The totals for the three days in Denver were 80,227, 65,261 and 66,987.

What a thrill to watch that huge crowd doing the wave. Cheering every pitch. Going berserk when Dale Murphy came to bat. My favorite play of the two games, besides Young's homer, was the suicide squeeze bunt by Freddie Benevides in the second game that brought home Joe Girardi. It came on a 2-2 pitch after Girardi had tripled. It gave the Rockies at 6-4 lead.

At the first game, I was crouched down by the home dugout about 10 feet from star Denver football player John Elway. He had about 12 cameras trained on him. I felt kind of sorry for the guy.

It was fun watching Dale Murphy come off the field after his opening hit. Murphy, who is a cinch Hall-of-Famer, could have slid into home base but chose to protect his fragile knees. He was thrown out and nobody complained. His career has been a class act and the crowd just loved him. It is obvious the team does, too.

MANY STARS EMERGED FOR THE ROCKIES. Second baseman Young was a huge hit. He and center fielder Alex Cole are fantastic and daring on the bases.

First baseman Andres Galarraga known as "Big Cat," is a great clean-up hitter and plays terrific defense. He runs the bases like Young and Cole, but, unfortunately, isn't as fast as the two smaller men.

Dante Bichette and Daryl Boston seem to platoon in the outfield and both are legitimate big leaguers. Boston comes to Colorado with real credentials while Bichette will establish his one game at a time.

Dave Nied and Bryn Smith will always be remembered for their winning pitching performances in those two opening games. That third game, when the Rockies lost 19-9, showed just how thin a pitching staff can be for an expansion team. Supposed ace reliever Steve Reed was pathetic. The Rockies needed help in the bullpen.

Charlie Hayes at third base, Freddie Benevides at shortstop and Joe Girardi at catcher made up a great infield. The team sure looked solid as those three team up with Young and Galarraga.

AFTER BEING VIRTUALLY SHUT OUT in their first two games at New York against two former Cy Young winners, Doc Gooden and Bret Saberhagen, Rockies fans wondered if the local boys could hit at all. That was answered substantially as the Rockies scored 29 runs in three games. They showed tremendous promise as hitters.

On Saturday, five of us headed to the ball park. Our group included my sons-in-law, Denny Haulman of Denver and Jerry Johnson of Winner, S.D. plus son Michael and former Lander residents, Don Sniffin of Boulder and Ron Sniffin of Laramie, my twin kid brothers.

We could only get $5 tickets, which I assumed would be somewhere in the stratosphere. They weren't. The seats were in the first upper deck above left field, and they were wonderful. It shows what a bargain tickets to Rockies games can be. It was a real family experience.

So far, I think the Rockies lead the majors with more than 28,000 season tickets sold. This might ensure that good tickets would be hard to find. Yet our experience was that good seats are available. And the Rockies even sell "rockpile" tickets for $1 each. Now you can't get much cheaper than that.

The grandstand was a sea of purple, black and white. The place was in a frenzy and it was an experience I will never forget.

Two

Fatherhood

Your children are not your children.
They are the sons and daughters
of Life's longing for itself.
They come through you
but not from you,
And though they are with you,
yet they belong not to you.
—*Kahlil Gibran, The Prophet*

Climbing Michael's mountain

As we sat there on that stone ledge,
I thought about sitting at my desk
just an hour earlier
wishing I were in this spot.

A SUNDAY AFTERNOON SEVEN YEARS AGO found me busy sitting at this desk at the *Journal*. And although the weather was beautiful outside, there was work to be done inside.

While I worked, it was impossible to not keep looking out the window. The beautiful Lander weather beckoned to me. Work was impossible. My output just kept getting slower and slower. The sun was shining on a beautiful Sunday afternoon in Lander. Yet here I was, inside my office, pounding on the keys of a computer terminal.

I picked up the telephone and called home. My then five-year-old son, Michael, answered the phone. He was just loafing.

"There's nothin' to do," he told me.

"How about going on a hike with me?" I asked him.

"Gee, Dad, that would be great!" he answered.

That was it for work. Enough of this sweatshop. I shut off my computer, turned out the lights, locked the front door, jumped in my car and headed home. We were ready for a Sunday afternoon adventure. We were going on a hike.

MY SON MET ME AT THE DOOR. He was wearing his favorite hat, jeans and boots. He already had a backpack loaded with food, soda pop and apples. He had my binoculars in his hand.

We live three miles from Lander just off Squaw Creek Road. There is a large red, rock-covered hill that towers over the homes in our subdivision. It doesn't have a name, but it looms several hundred feet above the land around. I pointed at the hill and said, "What do you think? Should we climb it?"

So off we went, a father and his son, heading for the boy's first big climb.

WE HAD TO WATCH FOR RATTLESNAKES, which occasionally cross through the Squaw Creek country.

"Dad, tell me about when you bricked that rattlesnake on our land," Michael asked me.

"Well, Son, it wasn't that big a deal. Our dog stirred one up, and I killed it with a brick."

"Don't you think maybe we should take some bricks along just in case we see a rattlesnake?" he asked.

"No, there are plenty of rocks we can use."

As we worked our way through the sagebrush, our house got smaller and smaller behind us and our destination got bigger as we approached it. Soon, we couldn't see the summit, just the huge red walls in front of it.

Michael wore his backpack, and I carried the binoculars, a camera and a walking stick. We wore caps to protect us from the bright sun. I wore a cowboy hat, and Mike had a camouflaged hat with a label that read "Mondak Pesticide." It was a gift from his grandpa. Michael calls it his "army cap."

Occasionally, we came upon odd-looking rocks. "Are these dinosaur bones, Dad?" He bent over and picked one up. "Sure looks like one to me." Every rock looks like a dinosaur bone to a five-year-old.

WE ARRIVED AT THE FIRST HURDLE. A large wall of red rock circled the big hill. It would take some looking to find a route through it.

After considerable exploring, we found a notch and soon we were through and standing on top of it. The view was splendid. The homes in our subdivision were now quite a bit below us and our view of the Sinks Canyon area was more detailed.

It was time for a soda pop break. As we sat there on that stone ledge I thought about sitting at my desk just an hour earlier wishing I were in this place. But our rest was short-lived.

"C'mon, Dad, let's go."

We circled around the hill that, by now, was known in my mind as Michael's Mountain, until we came to a gradual grade up the south side. We walked up through some more rock formations until we reached the biggest wall of rock. The eroded shapes were uniform as they stretched out of sight around the hill. There didn't appear to be an easy way through it except to climb. Not wanting to do that, we hiked around the hill until we reached a notch where fence posts had been laid in, I supposed, to keep cows from passing through.

"Indians must have done that, huh, Dad?" my son asked.

"No, probably a rancher a long time ago," I replied.

We were able to climb through the notch and get above the ledge. This was the last ledge we would face. The rest of the climb would just be a march up the steep, grassy hillside.

"Well, Son, the top is in sight. Are you ready for this final push?" He drew a deep breath and looking very serious assured me that, yes, he was ready for this final, big push to the summit.

The view got even better. We could see all the way to the Central Wyoming College campus in Riverton. The mountains behind the foothills of the Wind River Mountains were poking their peaks up into our view as we climbed.

EVERYWHERE AROUND US was down. Michael took off his backpack and we drank some pop, taking in a marvelous 360-degree view. The sun was still shining brightly and there was little wind.

There was noise from my neighbors working in their yards, and a rancher was running a tractor in a field off to the east. Smoke curled up from Lander in the distance as someone was burning out a ditch. The sky was typical Lander blue, and there were few clouds.

"Does it get any better than this?" I asked my son.

He wasn't listening. "Are you sure this isn't a dinosaur bone?" he asked.

"Maybe," I replied, which was the wrong thing to say. Soon, he had four huge bone-shaped rocks piled next to his backpack to take home.

We took some pictures and munched on our lunch. We scanned the horizon with the binoculars. It looked as if some rain clouds were forming over Fossil Mountain deep in Sinks Canyon. After about 30 minutes, the wind started to kick up. It was probably time to go home.

While we were sitting there, I turned to my son and asked him if he was going to remember this hike.

"I sure am, Dad. All my life!"

And so will I. All my life, too.

My daughter heads to school

Now it's the world's turn.
Today, we are trusting you to do
what is right for this little girl.

I T'S BEEN FIVE YEARS of diapers, doll houses, skinned knees, pony tails, Barbie dolls, tricycles, sparklers, double-runner ice skates, Big Wheels, kittens and hamsters.

Today, I'm turning over to the world my youngest child. Today is her first day of school.

She leaves our nest and finds out there's much more to life than just that which she's learned from her folks.

For five years now, she's believed that anything I told her was true. That all facts emanate from Dad. I've been her hero and her world has revolved around me, her mother, and her two older sisters.

Now it's the world's turn. Today we are trusting you to do what is right for this little girl. This five-year-old, who is so precious to us, and yet is just like thousands of other little five-year-olds.

I suppose there are dozens of other little girls with blond hair and blue eyes right here in Lander.

BUT, I'D LIKE A LITTLE EXTRA CARE taken with this one.

You see, this is our baby. This is the one I call "pookie" when she's good and "silly nut" when she's bad. This is the last of my girls to still always want a piggy-back ride.

And, this little girl still can't ride a bike. And she stubs her toe walking in sagebrush! She's afraid of the dark. And she doesn't like being alone.

Although she's quite shy, she is a friendly little girl. She's smart, I think. And she wouldn't hurt a flea.

I'll tell you what kind of kid this is.

Twice in the past month, she's come to me crying because the cat had killed a chipmunk. She buried both chipmunks side-by-side. She made little crosses for them, too.

This is the one who called the stars "dots," and once, when we were watering the yard, she commented on how we were "washing the grass."

She's just five years old. I'm trusting her fate now in the world's hands, and I'm judging that you'll be careful with her. She's a fragile thing in some ways, and in other ways, she's tough as nails.

She's not happy unless her hair is combed just right, and she might change her clothes five times a day. She likes perfume, too.

She also likes to play with toy race cars.

This is the one who always called pine trees "pineapple" trees. And when we visited Iowa, and she saw the huge fields of corn, she said "what big gardens they have here."

AND LIKE THOUSANDS OF OTHER LITTLE GIRLS, she's marching off to her first day of school this week.

And I know how those other parents feel, too.

There's a tightness in their chests. Their worlds seem a little emptier. The days are a little longer.

And when Amber comes home at the end of the school day, waving papers and laughing about the great time she had at school...when she tells us about the stars...and pine trees...and how the farmers raise crops, well...

She'll have grown up quite a bit already.

And I'll have grown a little older too.

A few of my favorite places

We all need to sit on "thinkings rocks" occasionally to help keep our lives in perspective.

I VISITED A FEW OF MY FAVORITE PLACES recently. I would like to share my experiences with you.

Lander's City Park always ranks high as a wonderful place to spend a sunny Sunday afternoon. The huge cottonwood trees provide ample shade, making that a cool place to enjoy a July afternoon.

The company was excellent that day when the local Legion Post put on their annual summer picnic. They had a nice-sized crowd who enjoyed the burgers, hot dogs, potato salad and other fixings.

My travels have taken me all over Wyoming. I would consider Lander's City Park as the most beautiful in the state. The park is in great shape. My compliments to Don Reynolds and his crew.

AFTER THAT WE HEADED UP TO SINKS CANYON. We have a favorite place, which really isn't all that secret — it is informally called Boulder Beach.

This is an area just down river from the bridge at the old Ski Area campground. There are four huge boulders in the middle of the river and you can easily scamper over to them and sunbathe or just relax and listen to the roar of the river.

They also provide a chance to "jump rocks" — a sport introduced to us by my brother John from Minneapolis and his two sons. They loved to practically run up and down the Popo Agie River jumping from rock to rock. I am not good at it, probably because of my conservative nature. I would not like to slip and fall. Then again, perhaps age has something to do with that attitude.

We didn't jump too many rocks that Sunday afternoon. We just sat around and enjoyed the scenery.

My son Michael kept asking me if I had located a perfect "thinking rock" and I told him, "Yes, I had." Ever since he was little, we have always sought out a thinking rock whenever we go hiking.

Boulder Beach is that perfect place where you sit on a rock and take in all that beauty around you. I would recommend it to others, too. We all need to sit on thinkings rocks occasionally to help keep our lives in perspective.

We watched a fly fisherman work the river. He didn't catch any fish, that we could see, but he had a heck of a good time. The campground was full of visitors. People were friendly and enjoying themselves. It was a cool place on a very hot day.

Further down the canyon, the river roars into a huge cavern on the east side. There is a gaping opening in the wall in the mountainside and the river thunders down over thousands of boulders and disappears right before your eyes into the ground. A quarter mile down the canyon, it reappears on the west side of the canyon. Some of the biggest trout you will ever see thrive in that big, calm pool where the river reappears.

On the way out of the canyon, the herd of bighorn sheep was hanging out near the road. They looked pretty mottled and we were surprised to see them down this low at this time of year.

T HEN WE MADE A TRIP TO FORT WASHAKIE and visited the Chief Washakie Plunge. People were thoroughly enjoying themselves in the mineral spring.

The facility is first class, and it was catering to dozens of people. The tribes, which own it, plan to soon add jacuzzi-type jets to the private baths to provide an improved experience.

Although we didn't swim this trip, we did enjoy the area. We had bought a pizza at the Shoshone-owned Tribal Texaco in Fort Washakie and ate it at the picnic area near the Plunge. We plan to go swimming there soon.

THESE ARE A JUST A FEW of my favorite places. I think you would like them, too.

25 and counting

The trouble with wedlock is that there's not enough wed and too much lock.
— *Christopher Morley*

TUESDAY WAS NANCY'S AND MY 25th wedding anniversary. How could the time have passed by so quickly?

That Morley joke at the start of this column is one of my favorites, but it really doesn't describe our marriage.

This quarter century together has been the best years of my life. Time does fly by when you are having a good time. I can't imagine how I would have had such a wonderful life without my wife and best friend.

I·can vividly remember that wedding day, wondering what is going to happen to us? It was a sunny, muggy day in western Iowa. I was 20 and my bride was 19. There was no way then of predicting all the things that have happened to us since that day in 1966.

AS I LOOK BACK on these years, I see a number of great things happening to us. It was Nancy's prompting that led us to move to Lander, Wyoming in 1970, a decision we've never regretted. This community has been mighty good to us and our family.

Our marriage has been blessed by four children. Our oldest, Alicia, is married to Dennis Haulman of Wheat Ridge, Colorado, and they have two little girls, Mallory and Mae.

Second daughter Shelli is a graduate of the University of Montana and is publisher, with her husband Jerry, of a newspaper that we own in Winner, South Dakota.

Youngest daughter Amber is going to college in Denver but wants to move to Texas in the near future.

That leads us to Michael, whose arrival in 1981 was a wonderful shock. This boy's role in our family has resulted in our meeting a whole new set of parents who also have elementary children. It's also given me the opportunity of participating in Cub Scouts and Little League.

As we sorted through the 25th wedding anniversary cards we've received, Nancy pondered all the cards like those she had sent out over the years. "As I recall, they were all mailed to old people!" she said.

BEN FRANKLIN HAD THIS TO SAY about marriage as a natural state for men and women:

Marriage is the proper and natural state of man. In it you will find solid happiness. It is man and woman united that makes the complete human being. Separate she wants his force of body and strength of reason, he her softness, sensibility and acute discernment. Together they are most likely to succeed in the world. A single man is an incomplete animal, he resembles the odd half of a pair of scissors.

IN THE RUSH OF OUR DAY-TO-DAY HURRYING, our 25 years together remind me of this favorite story:

There was a businessman who was having a birthday party for his wife of 25 years. In his haste, he forgot to order a cake.

At the last minute, he phoned the bakery, and some guy answered who told him all the decorators had gone home so there was no way to have a cake with specific lettering on it.

The businessman was frantic. "Could you just take any old cake and put some letters on it yourself?"

The guy answered that he probably could. "What do you want it to say? And where do you want the letters?"

"Just put *'you're not getting older'* on the top and *'you're getting better'* on the bottom line."

After work, the businessman was running late, but he rushed over to the bakery and picked up the cake and headed home in time to greet the guests. As he proudly unveiled the cake, there written on the top of it was the following:

You're not getting older on the top,
You're getting better on the bottom!

(Note: This column was written on May 10, 1991, on the occasion of our 25th wedding anniversary)

Our sonshine

Some people call a late pregnancy
like this a mixed blessing.
But even with more than an average
amount of complications, we never
viewed it as anything but the greatest
thing that had ever happened to us.

TWELVE YEARS AGO, our lives changed forever.

Our son Michael entered our world. After raising three daughters, Nancy and I finally had our boy. And his trip into this life was a most complicated one.

We had not expected to have any more children. Due to surgery prompted by some medical complications, the odds of us having another child were one in 5,000. That makes this a boy who wanted to come into this world pretty badly. He was our miracle baby.

Some people call a late pregnancy like this a mixed blessing. But even with more than an average amount of complications, we have never viewed it as anything but the greatest thing that has ever happened to us.

Besides being unplanned, Nancy had had some X-ray procedures at the very onset of the pregnancy that had us worried sick throughout the nine months. We had even been warned by doctor friends that things might not work out. This made the pregnancy seem like one of the longest in history.

What a thrill it was during that first ultrasound when we could see what appeared to be a healthy baby inside.

Pardon me for gloating, but I am still tickled about this whole event. And in some ways it may have been predicted.

Two weeks before we found out Nancy was pregnant, I bought a BB gun at an auction, for what reason, I had not the faintest idea. I think of that every time we shoot cans with that gun now.

When Michael headed off to kindergarten, I wrote the following column about my feelings on that great day. It went something like this:

THERE MUST BE MILLIONS OF LITTLE BOYS trooping off to their first day of school today.

Even here in Lander, there must be dozens of tousle-haired, freckle-faced little guys like our Michael heading to kindergarten.

This is a big moment in this little boy's life. And it's a big moment for his parents, too.

And like all those little boys and girls out there, he has been a special addition to our family. This is a kid who likes "smashed" potatoes. He thinks good athletes drink plenty of "Gator-egg" and he calls shooting stars "medium risers."

He started soccer and baseball this year, and it was a struggle at times. He said he liked tie games because "then nobody loses." During soccer it looked like his favorite play was eating orange slices during intermission.

His uncle Roger Thomsen took him fishing for the first time on a small lake in Iowa when he was four. The lake was full of little fish. The plan was to let Michael catch a fish, then throw it back in. Then catch another. Throw it back. And so on.

After this happened about the third time, Michael looked up at Roger and said: "Boy, that sure is a dumb fish!" He thought it was the same fish that he was catching each time.

ONCE, WITH HIS GRANDPA SNIFFIN, he mentioned that his best buddy Lyle was "sick."

Grandpa said that was too bad. "No, Grandpa, I said Lyle was sick."

Grandpa said, "Well, did he go to the doctor?"

"Grandpa, I said Lyle was sick! You know. One, Two, Three, Four, Five, SICK!"

He can be a brave little boy who, while walking down a dark mountain trail at night, would tell me, "I'm not afraid of the dark," all the while, tightening his grip on my hand.

He is just like all those other kids out there who are bravely marching off to school today, leaving their fathers and mothers to wonder just how could time pass so quickly?

Little boys like pets. He had a dog once that gave him a bad scrape around the eye. We were afraid he had lost his eye, but luckily there was no permanent damage. With boys, I'm afraid there may be more pets. This is a kid who picked up the nickname "Nutmeg" early and almost kept it. He outsmarted his sisters by giving away that name to his kitten. He used to have a big, black pet crow called Ronald Raven.

His uncle Rod is his godfather and, thus, is known as "Rodfather" by Michael.

He and his buddy Lyle skin up their knees a lot. And after seeing how they climb rocks, I understand why. Although they give me a heart failure sometimes when I see how high they climb.

They are fearless explorers. They also hunt rattlesnakes. Luckily, so far, it's only been hunting, not finding.

Yes, little boys are different from little girls.

So when our son comes home from school today he'll have grown a little older already. He'll have that big grin on his face and be waving papers and laughing...when he tells me about meteorites, Gatorade and mashed potatoes, plus a whole lot of other things, well...I'll know our baby isn't quite the baby he was when he left our house this morning.

WELL, WE ALL SURVIVED KINDERGARTEN. As he has grown, this boy has taught me patience in fishing and other father-son pursuits. I have even helped coach Little League the past five seasons. We go hunting and snowmobiling. He makes me feel young.

For his birthday, we had a cake decorated with baseball players. He got a new bike and a bike helmet among other things. His sisters loaded him down with baseball cards and Nintendo games. His aunt Susan Kinneman from Dubois recently returned from Japan, and she brought him a headband that makes him look like the Karate Kid IV. Susan celebrates her birthday on the same day as Michael's.

All in all, it has been among the best 12 years of my life. What a kick it has been to have this boy become a part of our lives.

A rainbow of feelings

I think there is a special place in a father's heart where his little girl's memories and good feelings reside. A father loves his daughter in a very special way.

THERE IS A SCENE in a recent movie where the dad gladly escorts his daughter down the aisle on her wedding day, and just as he is about to give her away, he realizes that he really is giving her away. He realizes that things will never be the same between him and his little girl again.

Well, that occurred to me in real life on a Saturday night in August when our daughter Shelli got married in Missoula, Mont.

And it was scary.

Not that I didn't have some experience at it. I went through this same thing a year ago in Denver when our oldest daughter, Alicia, got married. But you really can't understand what it feels like until it happens to you.

I ASKED SHELLI if I could say a few words at some point during her wedding ceremony. Here's what I said:

All fathers who have given away daughters know how I feel today. I feel happy, but I also feel a little sad.

This is the second summer in a row where Nancy and I have seen one of our daughters get married and establish a home of her own.

Now, today it is Shelli's turn.

I think there is a special place in a father's heart where his little girl's memories and good feelings reside. A father loves his daughter in a very special way.

My heart is a little mushy today. When I look into my heart I remember this very competitive little girl who could run faster and jump higher than any little girl I had ever seen before.

And she had a way of pestering me for things. She will always carry the title of Little Miss Nag in our family. She would blink those lashes of hers at me and I would give in, much like her advertising clients give in today. I suppose it was inevitable that she would end up in sales.

AS PARENTS, we gave our children roots. And we gave them wings.

It has been said that an eagle is safe in its nest. But that is not what an eagle is supposed to do. An eagle should soar, up among the rainbows.

Shelli is like that. She is made for flying and I am sure that, with Jerry by her side, they will soar high.

As for today's weather (it was snowing, in August!), I might add that it takes a little rain to make a rainbow. (Their wedding theme was the rainbow.)

Isn't it ironic that people in Jerry's family and people in our family describe these two in much the same ways? They are both always upbeat. They are athletic. They are so caring. They are the ones who provide inspiration to the rest of us. Perhaps it is not so surprising that they found each other and have chosen to spend the rest of their lives together.

TODAY IS A DAY to remember. It is a historic day for our family as we lose a daughter and gain a son.

We welcome Jerry into our family. He is a special person. For the second year in a row, we add to our family. Alicia's husband Denny Haulman joined our family a year ago, and it has been wonderful.

God bless you all.

A cross at Christmas

As we marched up the hill, we took note of the creek, the car and the road getting smaller beneath us. Also, our view of the vast Wind River Mountains kept getting better as we climbed.

T HE IDEA OF CREATING A CHRISTMAS CROSS on top of Crumps Moun-tain was not in our original plan. All we wanted to do was explore the Squaw Creek area that December Saturday afternoon and perhaps check out some deer.

We had lived at our home near Squaw Creek outside of Lander since June, 1976, and, although we had always enjoyed the view of Crumps Mountain, we had never set foot on that property. It was now time to do so and the excellent weather on that Saturday was perfect for it.

We left at 2:18 p.m. I believe the Denver Broncos were ahead 7-0, and darn it, I wanted to see the rest of that game! But my young son had pulled this promise out of me that we would take this hike, so away we went.

Our trip would take us across a large pasture and follow deer tracks until we could jump over the creek. Our original intentions weren't to climb the hill (or mountain, as Michael referred to it), but just to take a hike.

The day was glorious, about 30 degrees, no wind, and sunshine.

We followed the deer tracks to the creek and tried to find a way over. The creek was just a little too wide for my son's six-year-old legs. Finally, we found a deer-crossing zone, revealed by their tracks.

We were originally going to hike down the creek, but he didn't want to. He wanted to climb straight up. As we marched up the hill, we took note of the creek, the car and the road getting smaller beneath us. Also, our view of the vast Wind River Mountains kept getting better as we climbed.

We saw lots of tracks, mainly those of deer, in the red dirt. Crumps Mountain is a huge long butte made up of red dirt, red rocks, evergreen trees and unique benches of smooth rock that stretch horizontally for miles.

Occasionally, the snow was about 18 inches deep, and, at other times, the snow was gone and red mud stuck to our boots. The contrast of green bushes, white snow and red rocks was striking. The sun was peeking through the clouds just off the towering Wind River Mountains to our left.

WE CLIMBED ABOUT TWO THIRDS of the way up the hill where we found a nice place to rest. My son decided we should mark this place as it probably was going to be as high as we were going. He was getting tired. Slogging through the mud had taken its toll on us.

We stacked up some old dead wood in a pile and hoped that we could spot it with a telescope or binoculars from our kitchen window across the way.

Seven deer were crossing the creek where we had crossed it. They hopped across the field over to the north entrance to our Boulder Loop drive, jumped the fence and headed up to our neighbor's house, where they usually have some feed scattered around in the wintertime for their horses.

We spotted a trail that led up the mountain going the other way. It was a deer trail. So we followed the tracks, and it switch-backed the rest of the way up. Just like that, we were on top! We had climbed Crumps Mountain.

Our view was a panorama of most of the Lander Valley to the north, Table Mountain to the east, the Wind Rivers to the south and Red Butte to the west.

We saw two beautiful little birds chattering around in the 5- foot-high evergreens. They were multiple colors — white, gold, dark blue, etc. This was the day of the local Audubon bird count...perhaps we should have participated.

We climbed on over the mountain ridge toward the southwest and came into a clearing almost exactly north of our home. We each found a "thinking rock," which is my name for those rocks that are perfect for sitting on and thinking. I sat, while Michael immediately got up and wandered around. There would be little sitting for him this day. He was too excited. Any thought of exhaustion on his part disappeared once we got to the top.

I dragged a flat rock up to the top of the clearing and said we would use that as a marker, but he wasn't satisfied. Instead, he wanted to tear out a root, but couldn't quite coax it out of the ground.

I tugged at it and was surprised to see that it broke loose. So there I stood with a 10-foot long white root. We could use it for a marker. So without thinking, I placed it vertically against a dead tree there in a clearing on the top of the mountain. Would this work?

Michael disagreed, and not really realizing what we were doing, he insisted we lay it out horizontally, which we did. And it suddenly became a cross. We decided to call it our Christmas Cross.

THE SUN STARTED TO GO UNDER A CLOUD and the warmth disappeared. As we shivered, we looked down at our house and decided it was time to head home. The trip didn't take long at all. Little boys like to get muddy, and it was difficult keeping this boy from getting dirty from head to toe.

I kept looking back to see if our cross was visible, but it wasn't — to us, anyway, from that angle.

Once home, we got out the telescope and scanned the tops of the mountain from our kitchen window. And there it was. We had gone all the way up there. It was our little way of celebrating Christmas.

Our little trip certainly didn't measure up to all the good charitable works people around Lander did that day delivering Christmas baskets and so forth, but it will go down in our memories as the day we climbed Crumps Mountain and created a Christmas Cross.

I don't remember a thing about what the Denver Broncos did on that Sunday afternoon, but that cross will live forever in my memories.

A family monologue

—————⇒►◦◄⇐—————

Many family legends and stories are based around this tendency to blow our tops. I come from a family of 11 kids and perhaps we formed a pretty good lab experiment of such things.

—————⇒►◦◄⇐—————

BACK ON JULY 4, 1988, members of our family gathered together in Lander for a family reunion. It was the first time in 15 years that all 11 children had gotten together at the same time with the parents and all the grandchildren.

I hosted the event in Lander and emceed the event. These are some observations I made to my siblings and their families during a time when we all took the microphone and shared our family memories:

THAT FIRST CAR: My first real experience with a custom car was our family's purchase of a 1950 Oldsmobile 88. It was a four-door and was some sort of gray and rust color.

My older brother Tom had his driver's license and got to drive this car. We loved it. It had power, and, for all practical purposes, it was ours.

One day, we decided to customize it. But what we really wanted to do was have it painted. In checking around, the prices were just too high.

Finally ,we decided to do it ourselves. Since we didn't know how to spray paint, and we didn't have the equipment, it seemed logical to paint it with brushes.

I picked out the color — it would be bright red. I'll never forget that Saturday afternoon. The car was parked beside the family gas station, and Tom and I, each armed with a bucket of bright red paint and our brushes, started to paint the car.

Our buddies all came by and admired it. Most of them were younger than Tom — about my age, probably 12 to 14. It really sparkled when it was done. We had transformed that old gray beast into this magnificent red machine.

We were a little disappointed, though, when we heard the big guys from downtown asking if "we had painted it with a broom!" It became known as the "squirrel-tail custom" of our family, which was the unkindest cut of all in Wadena, Iowa, in the spring of 1959.

Squirrel-tail custom was the type of description used to describe a car that somebody very cheaply tried to customize. You really didn't do the job right if you didn't spend much time or money on the project.

I would suppose the ultimate squirrel-tail custom would involve putting a squirrel tail on your antenna, and that was it. We had done a little better, though, we had painted our old four-door car with a broom!

MY FORD: We did better later on though. A week before my 16th birthday, my dad announced he had acquired a heck of a car. It was a 1951 Ford Victoria, two-door hardtop. Now this was a car!

Uncle LeRoy Brockmeyer had found it and made a deal with dad, and it was soon coming to us. I immediately claimed it as my own.

Since I was working a lot at the station in those days, Dad let me customize it in the grease bay. If I recall, my salary during the summer (working full-time) was $25 per week and all the gas I could burn. Not bad.

I wanted to paint, shave, deck and rake this car. And I also installed drag pipes and some other kind of pipes that hung below the rear axles.

A family friend painted the car a glossy black — this time with a spray gun.

The result of all this was a gorgeous car. I wish I still had it. It was great. It had a flat-head V8 engine with a "three on the tree" stickshift and overdrive. I ultimately put the shift on the floor, striped the dashboard black and white, puttied in all the hood, removed the grill, shaved the deck (cleared off all the chrome from the trunk lid) and filled it in. You popped open the trunk by opening a converted hood latch located just under the left rear tail light.

The rear end of the car stood high in the air. We turned the leaf springs upside down, giving it a "raked" effect. I always figured it would get good gas mileage since I was always going downhill.

Somewhere along the way, I found somebody's discarded lakes pipes. These were long chrome jobs that ran alongside the rocker panels of the car. I cut them down and extended them from the mufflers on my new dual exhausts. Thus, they ran under the axle and blew exhaust straight out.

So there I was. I suddenly had one of the best looking cars in the county. I was just 16 and had unlimited gasoline. Had I died and gone to heaven, or what? My buddies (Neal Jennings and others) and I would cruise the county, but we had very poor luck picking up girls.

Even then I was conservative; I wasn't into driving hell-bent, or driving drunk or drag racing. I was all show, not go. I left the engine virtually the same as always.

Little did I realize that my car was getting noticed. I was told later that I was becoming known around Northeast Iowa as that kid from Wadena with the neat Ford Victoria two-door hardtop.

THE SMELL OF GAS: It seems to me that the smell of gasoline will be with me all my life.

We grew up in a family that dealt in gas. Perhaps this is much like a farm family that seemed to smell of cows or pigs all their lives. Somehow you never forget that smell.

My dad worked in the gasoline business for 45 years. After he got out of World War II, he started driving a gas truck and he spent much of the rest of his life running a bulk plant, gas stations and driving a gas truck.

My eight brothers and I all got to enjoy climbing on Dad's gas truck when he filled it at the bulk plant and went to farms and contractors and filled tanks.

Those memories of the smell of gas linger whenever I fill my car up at a self-service gas station. Those odors bring back memories of the smells we lived with as children growing up.

TEMPERS: One of the characteristics unique to members of my family is a ferocious temper. Is this an inherited characteristic or is a learned one?

Who cares?

Many family legends and stories are based around this tendency to blow our tops. I come from a family of 11 kids and perhaps we formed a pretty good lab experiment of such things.

There are nine boys and two girls in the family. And the temper problems seem to be confined to the boys. They are Tom 50, Bill 47, John 46, Pat 44, Jim 39, Dan 34, Jerry 31 and the twins Ron and Don, 30. The temperamental ones are easy to pick out, in order of the violence of their tempers:

Worst is Tom, followed by Dan, Jim and me. The others don't seem to have this characteristic. Isn't that odd?

I think we should rate these tempers. And since I am one of the persons involved, I can talk about this. And since we tend to make an arse of ourselves when it happens, the rating system I'm going to use is a ranking on the Sphincter Scale...much like a Richter scale for earthquakes.

Ron and Don rank 3.0 on the sphincter scale. Jerry, if he is partying, jumps from a 3.5 to a 7.0 really quickly. Dan is about 4.0 normally but has been known, according to his siblings, to erupt into a 9.5.

Tom probably hits 9.6 occasionally, as I have, along with brother Jim.

All-in-all, we aren't so bad.

Actually, these are pretty mellow fellows.

The reunion was great and people kept their tempers in check.

Father's Day memories

And I'm glad my dad is still alive
so I can share with you some of my
feelings for my father in this
Father's Day's message.

MY EARLIEST MEMORY is one of riding in my dad's big gas truck while bouncing down a gravel road in northeastern Iowa.

The scene was repeated a lot as I was growing up. It seemed my dad was always making deliveries, and it was a real treat if any of us kids got to go along. It also provided a moment of relief for my mother, as she contended with my younger brothers and sisters.

My father no longer drives a gas truck. He and my mother live north of Denver now. They are retired. I'm glad they are out West, too, so that I can share with them the wonders of living in The Best Part of America.

And I'm glad my dad is still alive so I can share with you some of my feelings for my father in this Father's Day's message.

We had a large family. There are nine boys and two girls. I was the second oldest. I think times were probably pretty hard back then, but we really never knew that. We certainly didn't miss any meals and always somehow got what we needed. The consensus in the family is that somehow we were all spoiled rotten, if such a thing could be possible.

My dad was always very well read. He would subscribe to lots of magazines and he read every evening. Often, he would read to us items that he found interesting on state, national and the international scene. We often debated various issues.

On labor issues, he was adamant. He was always a non-stop defender of the little guy.

Because of our large family, he always had to have two or three extra jobs and his days were long. Besides the tank wagon, he drove a school bus and sold insurance at night and on weekends.

He would explode in fury over the policies of the rich politicians for not caring more for the little guy. He was a liberal in a time and place when and where they were little appreciated. The war in Vietnam especially took its toll on his friendship with many people during the turbulent 1960s.

My brothers and I would go to school armed with arguments against the Vietnam war. There was one history teacher, Darryl Leonhardt, who politically was somewhat to the right of Attila the Hun.

Anyway, old Darryl would argue endlessly with us Sniffin kids. And since there were 11 of us, I'm sure he wondered if this march would ever end!

My dad spent three and a half years in Iran during the Second World War. That made him somewhat of an authority on that subject and he never tired of telling us stories about the Mideast and what a bunch of crazies he thought occupied that part of the world.

Disciplining nine sons would be hard for anyone. The four oldest boys slept in one big bedroom upstairs in our large home. Typically, we were making lots of racket one night. Repeatedly, Dad would holler at us and warn us that he was going to take off his belt and come up those stairs and whip us. Finally, he'd had enough of our shenanigans.

Slowly, we heard him sigh at the bottom of the stairs. Then we heard his belt come off with a slap. Then he slapped it a few times against his thigh. Then he slowly trudged up the stairs. We looked at each other in terror. It had finally happened — we'd gone too far and boy, were we going to get it!

But he wasn't so tough. It was mostly show. But it did get us to behave ourselves. We never even got a whipping that night.

MY DAD IS A VERY HONEST PERSON. He always emphasized that we must be truthful and never lie. For some reason, he always emphasized to me that I had never lied to him.

On one occasion when I was about 10, we boys had pulled some stunt. I don't remember now what it was, but I remember the aftermath like it was yesterday.

My dad called me aside and firmly told me, "Bill, I know you'd never lie to me. Now, look me in the eye and tell me what you boys have been up to."

I don't remember what I told him, but I do remember I looked him in the eye and I lied. That lie haunted me. Later, I told him the truth. I don't think he would have ever known that I had lied, but that wasn't nearly as important to me as the fact that I did.

I never forgot that incident and I think it tells something about my dad's character. Happy Father's Day, Dad.

Hey Dad, wanna play catch?

I think there is a bond between fathers
and sons that often comes out
in a shared sporting activity.

AS A FATHER, the words in this headline mean a lot to me.

The other day, my son Michael came bounding into the family room where I was reading a newspaper and said, "Hey Dad, wanna play catch?"

That was my cue to head outside and toss the football around with my 12-year-old son.

While we were throwing the ball, I reflected on that question he had asked me.

What a splendid situation. What if he didn't want to play catch with me? I'm sure there could be a day in the future when the old man won't be able to play a decent game of catch with an older teenager. Perhaps it won't be fashionable for a teen to be caught playing catch with dad.

It seems like we have been playing catch with footballs or baseballs for all his life with a lot of basketball shooting in between. How much have I enjoyed this? As much as anything in my life.

I think there is a bond between fathers and sons that often comes out in a shared sporting activity. Men, by nature, often keep their emotions inside. But the shared activity of throwing and catching a ball together probably rekindles some prehistoric bonding trait that occurred when fathers taught their sons how to hunt or how to scout.

I can't help but feel warm all over when I think about playing catch with my son.

WHEN I WAS GROWING UP, my dad wasn't able to play a lot of catch with me. Times were different back in the 1950s. I can recall a few times when my dad played catch with me. He would dig out this old-fashioned glove and it was great fun.

He had played a lot of ball and was a good player. I was always impressed at how well he could play — especially with a glove that looked flat as a pancake.

My dad always had at least three jobs, and since there were four of us older boys in the family, we really didn't need Dad around in order to have a game of catch. But I remember those games of catch with him clearly. I hope my dad remembers them, too.

A few years ago, I talked my dad out of that old glove, and I am faithfully saving it. I plan somehow to frame it and put it up on the wall as a monument of those times when a father plays catch with his son.

SO ANYWAY, I have to interrupt writing this column, which I am doing on a portable computer in my family room at home.

My son Michael just came bounding the room and...well, you know what he asked me. See you later.

Three

People

To laugh often and much;
to win the respect of intelligent people and
the affection of children; to earn the
appreciation of honest critics and endure the
betrayal of false friends; to appreciate beauty;
to find the best in others; to leave the world a
bit better, whether by a healthy child, a
garden patch or a redeemed social condition;
to know even one life has breathed easier
because you have lived.
This is to have succeeded.

— *Ralph Waldo Emerson*

The Real Marlboro Man

When he laughs, he squints his eyes and that crinkled look comes to his face that has looked down on a billion people from Hong Kong to Oslo to Cairo.

I HAD SEEN THAT FACE all over the world. In an airport in London. On billboards in Paris and Rome. You couldn't go anywhere in Tokyo or Taipei without seeing it.

The face. It is possible that this face is the most photographed face in the modern world. His face jumps out of ads in magazines and newspapers world wide. It could be easily argued that the sun never sets on his image.

And this man lives here in Wyoming. In fact, he lives just 25 miles from me, just outside of Riverton.

He's the Marlboro Man. And he's real. And he's a cowboy.

He is a quiet, laid-back guy. A horse trainer and horse trader. And he's one of us. Just a local Fremont County guy who thinks this is the greatest place to live in the world.

For 22 years, Marlboro has used his image to portray the "man's man" world portrayed by this cigarette. He is Darrell Winfield and he lives on a nicely-kept 40-acre spread six miles north of Riverton.

And he smokes Marlboros.

I HADN'T TALKED TO DARRELL for about 10 years, which had been too long. The idea to go see him came up when our Irish reporter visitor, Kevin Magee, was wondering about what stories he could do here that he might be able to use back in Belfast. When he lit up a Marlboro, I mentioned that the "Marlboro Man" lived here.

"Nah," he replied, "You're kidding." He continued to protest and said there really was no such person.

"Sure there is. And he lives here in Fremont County. He's a friend of mine," I told him.

So the Wednesday before Thanksgiving, we drove over to visit. Darrell's wife Linnie greeted us at the door. A pleasant, warm woman, she ushered us into the house and offered us coffee. Darrell was sitting back in an easy chair chewing the fat with two buddies, Willie and Tom.

After we were all introduced, Willie and Tom said, "Now, don't believe what he tells you. We'll tell the truth about him," which brought out a chuckle from Winfield.

For someone who has had more than 100,000 photos taken of him, the most prominent shot of him on the wall in the den was a series of photos showing Winfield getting thrown from a horse during one sequence. They all laughed recalling that incident.

When he laughs, he squints his eyes and that crinkled look comes to his face that has looked down on a billion people from Hong Kong to Oslo to Cairo.

I mentioned that during a trip to Taiwan this summer, I had seen thousands of billboards around Taipei with his face on them.

I was over there promoting travel for the state of Wyoming. We picked up some brochures from the biggest travel agency in Taiwan that had struck a deal with Marlboro to promote Wyoming as "Marlboro Country." Winfield agreed that it was a good idea and he wondered why the state had not pursued that before.

O NE OF THE PHOTOGRAPHERS who most often shoots the photos of Winfield walked into the room at this point in our conversation. He was Jack Ward of Philadelphia. He took his first photos of Darrell in 1968, when he first became the Marlboro man.

Darrell was providing the horses for the ads, and as a 38-year old cowboy with a chiseled face and crinkly eyes, he suddenly became an international symbol of manhood.

Ward tries to spend time at Big Sky in Montana where he has a cabin and he was invited to Darrell's place for Thanksgiving.

They laughed over some early picture assignments, and each complained about how hard it was to work with the other.

"I have been trying to tell the company to have the photographers pay for their own film," Ward said, about shooting so many photos of Winfield. "Then they wouldn't waste so much." Ward said they will often have 300 36-shot rolls at the end of a shooting. I suggested they measure the photos they took of Winfield in feet rather than shots. Ward said it would be more appropriate to measure it in miles. He says there are enough shots of the Riverton cowboy to stretch around the world. And indeed, they do stretch around the world in the way Marlboro has promoted the image.

WHAT KIND OF MAN IS WINFIELD? Could he live up to the macho image being sold by Marlboro?

In the setting we saw him, Winfield is the ultimate family man. He and his wife Linnie have six children and eleven grandchildren.

He was planning an annual trip the day after Thanksgiving to Rock Springs for a horse sale. He always takes his grandsons on this trip as a weekend "for the boys," as he called it. "They love it," he says. They go to the Outlaw Inn in Rock Springs, and the kids can swim and they go out to eat at night. He said his two young granddaughters have been clamoring to go along so finally grandma will go, too, to watch the girls.

He says the boys are complaining, but he feels it is only fair that the girls finally get to go, too.

On the subject of his wife, Winfield, an old horse trainer, says he has been training her for 40 years. "Ain't got her trained, yet, though," he laughed. Linnie looked over, smiled at that remark and offered us more coffee.

WITH THE SUN SLIPPING BEHIND THE HILL, we decided to go outside and snap some of our own photos. Jack came along and helped take some pictures. Darrell struck a classic pose, and Kevin and I took turns posing with him.

As we parted company and then headed back home, my Irish friend was still in a daze. "I still can't believe it. He lives. He really lives," he concluded with an amazed look on his face.

Schwarzkopf a field marshall in Wyoming

"I was hesitant to kill any of Dick Cheney's constituents. But then I aimed at an antelope and heard him say, 'Long live the Ayatolla,' which revealed to me that it was one of those subversive terrorist antelopes, so I felt okay in blasting him!"

GENERAL H. NORMAN SCHWARZKOPF, head of the Allied Forces in Operation Desert Storm, hunted quarry in the Wyoming desert in 1989 just as effectively as he hunted the Iraqi Army in the Arabian desert in the spring of 1991.

Schwarzkopf competed in the Lander One Shot Antelope Hunt with a team that included two other generals. He had such a good time, he had planned to return for the 1990 hunt, only to be detained by Operation Desert Storm.

The burly general, who is also known by his nicknames "Bear" and "Stormin' Norman," has been in world-wide news almost nonstop since the start of the desert campaign. His successful battle against the Iraqis has been hailed as one of the most successful military campaigns in all of history.

As PART OF THE ANNUAL ONE SHOT VICTORY BANQUET, team members stand up before the large crowd and tell true tales and sometimes tall tales about their hunt. As captain of his team, Schwarzkopf said about his hunt:

"I was hesitant to kill any of (then Secretary of Defense) Dick Cheney's constituents. But then I aimed at an antelope and heard him say, 'Long live the Ayatolla,' which revealed to me that it was one of those subversive terrorist antelopes, so I felt okay in blasting him!"

While at the Lander One Shot Hunt, he posed for a photo with Ceremonial Shoshone Chief Darwin St. Clair during special Indian ceremonies prior to the annual hunt. Other Shoshones involved in the event were John Tyler and Willie LeClair.

The Indian ceremony must have been effective. All three generals got their antelope with one shot apiece the following morning.

The three generals all scored kills, but didn't win the Hunt because of too much elapsed time. As a result, Schwarzkopf got to dance with the other losers, who included famed test pilot Chuck Yeager, actor Dale Robertson, custom car builder Carroll Shelby, plus two governors, three Congressmen and other notables. The winning team that year was captained by Wyoming Governor Mike Sullivan.

ONE SHOT PRESIDENT BILL GUSTIN received a note from the general after the 1989 Hunt which seemed to compare the hunt to one of his own well-run military operations. It read:

"Just a quick note to thank you for inviting me to participate in the One Shot Antelope Hunt. From the moment I arrived at the airport through the entire weekend in Lander, right up to the point when the plane departed, it was a great event that was executed without a flaw.

"Believe me when I say that I know that something like this does not happen by accident. It is always the result of detailed planning and months and months of hard work by a whole bunch of dedicated people.

"I applaud your leadership and the hard work of all the members of the One Shot Club in the success you achieved last weekend. Thank you for a splendid hunt. As a Past Shooter, I am proud to be affiliated with your organization. If I can be of assistance to you in any way, please do not hesitate to contact me."

SCHWARZKOPF DID RETURN TO LANDER in 1993 and headed another team of shooters.

He was a gracious visitor, posing for pictures and signing hundreds of autographs. He didn't get an antelope during the 1993 Hunt, let alone a shot during foggy, wet conditions.

"I did make a discovery, though," he told the delighted audience. "There is a new breed of antelope out there. I call it the Stealth Antelope."

Try
to imagine...

Try to imagine the pain these men felt as they died young, knowing their wives and kids would lead emptier lives because their husbands and fathers were not there. In many cases, the illnesses strained both the financial and emotional resources of these families to the breaking point.

TRY TO IMAGINE how it must feel to be on your deathbed knowing that your widow and children are going to live difficult lives without you. Try to imagine going to your grave with that feeling in your heart.

That is exactly what has happened in the case of more than 20 Fremont County men who have died prematurely of lung cancer. These men died terrible deaths as they gradually lost their ability to breathe. Many left young families with children still in school and left their widows to be both mother and father to these kids. This is the story of middle-aged uranium miners dying before their time.

Try to imagine the pain these men felt as they died young, knowing their wives and kids would lead emptier lives because their husbands and fathers were not there. In many cases, the illnesses strained both the financial and emotional resources of these families to the breaking point.

Try to imagine what it must have felt like to have been told you should not have been smoking, when most everyone around you smoked. And you thought this assumed harmless habit is what caused the lung cancer, not the radon gases you breathed as an underground uranium miner.

Try to imagine fatherless children and husbandless wives coping with the loss of the heads of their families. Imagine the sense of loss these people lived with through the loss of a loved one at a premature age.

And finally, as a dying miner, try to imagine your frustration when you learn that there might be some relief available except that proof is necessary and most of the records have been destroyed.

Imagine how you would feel when you find out you have been abandoned and now you will die.

To THOSE OF US who have been observers of this situation, those of us who never descended into a hot, dusty, dangerous uranium mine, the whole scenario listed above may seem remote. But to those miners and their families, the feelings described here are very real.

Many of the survivors of these dead miners are bitter. All are disappointed. Every one is sorrowful. All that hurt was so unnecessary because of a lack of safety precautions.

This country has shown it has a big heart for people who have been wronged. This is especially true when it can be argued that the government was partially at fault.

The COMMENTS ABOVE were written by me as an editorial in our newspaper during a campaign in the spring of 1990 to call attention to dying uranium miners.

The series *Why Did The Miners Die?* called attention to the odd type of cancer that was killing local men 20 years after they had descended into dangerous uranium mines.

Leading the charge was Mildred Olson, a Lander widow, whose husband Digger had died at a young age from complications of cancer.

She claimed that his body was so radioactive that grass wouldn't grow on his grave. She said tests on his bones showed he had 14 times the normal radiation in his body. He died a terrible death and left four small kids for Mildred to raise.

Her battle and the incredible efforts by U. S. Sen. Al Simpson resulted in Congress passing a bill, signed by President Bush, that offered a national apology to the men and paid them $100,000 each in benefits. Olson was the second person to receive such a check and another five have been paid so far.

Our series of articles won a Special Merit Award from the Wyoming Press Association for Investigative Reporting and a third place national award for the effort. Sen. Simpson wrote a letter in support of the series to win a Pulitzer Prize, which we did not win, however.

At a picnic held by former uranium miners in Riverton to celebrate the passage of the bill, the miners presented me with an old miner's helmet signed by all the miners or their widows.

And out of more than 200 state and national awards won by our newspaper, we are most proud of that simple, old, battered helmet.

The disaster business

I told him that I knew of a state in the Rocky Mountains that was suffering a similar fate.

MY WIFE NANCY AND I had settled into two seats of the British Airways flight from Rome to London back in 1986. I was sitting next to an impeccable-looking gentleman.

Often you make small talk at times like this. I was surprised by what he said to me.

"I'm in the disaster business," the stranger was telling me. Did he work for the CIA? Or for Khadafy? He looked too mild-mannered for either of those careers. Yet when I asked him what business he was in, that was his answer.

Finally, he smiled and said: "I'm in the oil business. Don't you think $10 a barrel is a disaster?" His name was Roland Schwab and he was commuting between the two European capital cities. He was vice-president of a Canadian energy conglomerate, and he handled its oil business in Europe and the Mideast.

He was a citizen of Switzerland but maintained dual residences in London and Rome. He said it had taken his company six months to move its office from London to Rome. "It all involves finding the right person who will make the right decision in order to get anything done in Italy," he said.

I told him that we knew a little about his disaster business, too.

I told him that Wyoming was also suffering in a big way because of the decline in oil prices. He said he knew all about our problems, as he formerly worked for Husky Oil and had been to Cody a number of times. "That was many years ago, though," he said.

HE OBSERVED THAT SHEIK YAMANI of Saudi Arabia was the smartest person in the region when it comes to oil. "He is the brains of the Mideast," he said. "He is professional and real sharp. He is a very pleasant guy, but I don't think even Yamani can get the Arabs to work together this time around.

"The Arabs have real problems," he continued. "All those nations have made huge commitments to their countries based on a certain amount of income coming in. It's the same as Mexico. When a nation's entire economy is based on oil at a certain price, well . . . there's going to be trouble when the prices drop this far."

I told him that I knew a state in the Rocky Mountains that is suffering a similar fate.

"On the bright side," he continued, "I heard an expert this week who claimed oil will soon be back up to $23 per barrel." I told him the folks back in Wyoming will be glad to hear that. Did he believe that? "No, unfortunately, I don't," he said, rather sadly, shrugging his shoulders. He expects $10 per barrel oil to continue for several months, maybe years.

SCHWAB SAID HE WAS VERY DISAPPOINTED in our country's actions in Libya. "You fell into Khadafy's trap," he said.

He said the other moderate Arab countries are compelled to support Libya in this struggle for the sake of unity. "The other leaders would like to see Khadafy overthrown, but when the U.S. is picking on Libya, the whole Libyan citizenry rallies behind Khadafy," he said.

"The whole thing makes Libya look like such an underdog. People over here can't help but wonder why the Americans are picking on such a poor little country like Libya," he said.

He reminded me that Italy is very supportive of Libya. "It's their former colony," he said. "The Italians have a very high emotional tie with Libya."

By then our flight had arrived in London. We said our farewells and I promised him I'd send him a copy of this column on his observations from across the world. His insights made our flight go by very quickly.

About my dentist

He is everything a good dentist should be except for this one bad habit.

A TRIP TO THE DENTIST is something that I try to put off as long as possible. Despite the new modern tools, all I can remember is the terrible pain connected with the dentist's chair that I experienced as a youngster.

Our family dentist (Walt Girgen) is a nice man. He appears to be very dedicated to his work, has a finely staffed office, and has brand-new equipment.

He is everything a good dentist should be except for this one bad habit.

Let's describe the situation.

Once in his office, we make the nervous small talk. I'm gripped with the same terror that always gripped me in a dentist's office as a child.

We talk a little about the weather and a little about the work that's going to be done. He asks if there's been any discomfort since the last time. There hasn't.

I get into the chair, and they adjust it so that I'm literally standing on my head.

Several clamps are inserted in my mouth, my gums are numbed and a round thing similar to a funnel is jammed into my mouth, so that it's as wide open as possible.

91

NOT ONLY CAN'T I TALK, but I can hardly breathe. This is when my dentist comes through with his bad habit. He starts asking questions.

"How are things down at the *Journal,* Bill?"

"Boy, that series on the school was really something. What do you have scheduled next on it?"

"I just bought a new camera. What kind of camera do you use at the *Journal?"*

"How old are you, anyway?"

"How is your book coming along?"

"Did you get your sheep?"

"Have you been flying much, lately?"

"You don't mind if I ask you these questions, do you?"

Tom Bell: Father of Wyoming's environmental movement

>=>=o=<=

Yet he kept on writing about saving the
Wyoming environment.
The ideas he proposed were good then,
and they are good now.
Tom Bell was a realist.

>=>=o=<=

A GENUINE HERO was honored in Lander recently. The Wyoming Outdoor Council presented its founder with a special award recognizing just what Tom Bell has meant to that organization.

Bell, a Lander native, literally lost the farm back in the early 1970s as he, almost single-handedly at times, attempted to bring some sense of reason and restraint to the rampant growth that was occurring in Wyoming.

A rancher, a teacher, a biologist, a botanist, an injured war veteran, a writer, an editor, a publisher and an environmentalist.

These words described Tom during a career that saw him move from a passive position to become one of the most visible people in Wyoming politics in the early 1970s.

Tom was there promoting these concepts when the Wyoming Outdoor Council was formed. His newspaper, the *High Country News,* was born in Lander in early 1970 and became the foremost environmental newspaper in the Rocky Mountain Region during the 1970s. It is currently being published in western Colorado.

The income to the newspaper was so small at times that Tom ultimately had to sell his beautiful ranch west of Lander in order to pay the paper's bills.

YET HE KEPT ON WRITING about saving the Wyoming environment. The ideas he proposed were good then, and they are good now. Tom Bell was a realist. He never advocated a monkey wrench approach to saving the environment.

The Wyoming legislature created some landmark laws during the 1970s including severance taxes, reclamation laws, plant siting regulations and the creation of councils for air and water quality. No doubt Tom's writings had an influence on these pieces of legislation.

There are a great many people in Wyoming who deserve a lot of credit for being so far-sighted in the need of such policies. But the man who deserves much of the credit, in our opinion, is Lander's Tom Bell.

A gentle man, he ultimately became burned out by the controversies. He and his wife Tommy took their three adopted children (their three natural children were raised) and moved to Oregon. He did some farming, some writing and some teaching.

He finally returned to Lander a few years ago and joined the staff of our newspaper as a reporter, specializing in historical material. Presently he is in charge of the historical magazine produced quarterly by the Pioneer Museum.

We were pleased to see Tom Bell honored by the Outdoor Council, and we join with them in congratulating this visionary man.

A eulogy for my friend Ross

Perhaps it is because I am a trained
reporter that I remembered so many
of these conversations.
I will try to share with you — all of you
who loved Ross like I did — what he
told me about the things he loved.

I WAS HONORED TO WRITE AND DELIVER a eulogy back in 1985 when my best friend, J. Ross Stotts, was killed in a car accident.

Highlights of that eulogy are included here. I could never have written a book without mentioning my late friend.

I'M STANDING HERE looking out at all the people who loved Ross. And let me tell you, he loved all of you.

Outside of his wife Joy, I was privileged to have more conversations with Ross in the last three years than anyone else. We were partners in several ventures in South Dakota. We had become the best of friends. I miss him terribly.

I spent hundreds of hours talking with Ross during our trips to South Dakota. Perhaps it is because I am a trained reporter that I remember so many of these conversations. And that's why I'm here. I will try to share with you — all of you who loved Ross like I did — what he told me about the things he loved.

To his wife Joy, Ross told me a hundred times of how much he loved you and how happy he'd been since you two got married. When we were away, he missed you terribly. He couldn't wait to call you and tell you we'd made the trip safely in the airplane.

To Ross's sons, Mike and Mark, I can tell you he loved and cared deeply for you. But you'd be so proud to hear how he talked about you. Mike, you look so much like your dad, I feel like I know you well. Mark, your dad told me repeatedly that he regretted that you and he didn't have more time together these last few years.

Ross was a man's man. He was a true Western man. He loved to wear cowboy boots and a fancy cowboy hat. He even got me wearing cowboy boots and a cowboy hat for a while.

Our Spearfish publisher Bill Kunerth told me that the staff over there referred to Ross and me as Butch Cassidy and the Sundance Kid. I told Ross I thought we looked like Kenny Rogers and Snuffy Smith. Actually, I called him "Rosco" and he called me "Billy Bob."

PERHAPS A REAL MAN isn't supposed to show love. But Ross did. Those around him knew he was a man who cared for other people. He had a great compassion for people. Bill Kunerth said it very well: "When you were around Ross, you felt better about yourself."

Ross and I were a team. We both had full-time jobs in Lander but I also had this three-newspaper operation 375 miles away. With Ross's help, we operated a satellite dish store, a press company and had construction permits for three low-power TV stations.

We were partners with Brian Miracle in a great airplane, a Cessna 182. Ross and I would fly over to South Dakota on weekends. We were fortunate to have good staffs there. Many of those people are here today.

Ross was a CPA and a great accountant. He would get upset with me, though, if I would pigeonhole him on some deal as if he were the bookkeeper. He would remind me of his extensive business experience and took exception to being considered just an accountant.

We called ourselves Mr. Inside and Mr. Outside. Our system worked well, and, frankly, I'm at a loss of how I'll get along without him. He was good, and I complimented him often. He'd often reply to me: "You know, I didn't ride in here on a load of watermelons."

ALTHOUGH ROSS was an extremely hard worker and very capable, he also thought all work and no fun was a mistake. He slowed me down a lot and used to tease me about my "running in place" approach to work. He taught me racquetball and golf, two sports at which he was outstanding. He also tried to teach me how to take a pinch of Skoal, but I just couldn't master it.

HE WAS AN AVID PILOT. We flew hundreds of hours together. He had become an outstanding and safe pilot. Some of the windy, short South Dakota airstrips we flew into made him an even better pilot.

Our joke was that "we cheated fate one more time" whenever we'd made a typical cross-wind South Dakota landing.

I had an eerie situation happen yesterday. I visited the funeral home and saw Ross's body for the first time since the accident. It was a very difficult time for me. Lots of thoughts raced through my head as I spent those moments alone with him.

Our flights together were heavy on my mind as I got up and went outside. An airplane was coming in for a landing right over the funeral home. It was Ross's and my airplane. Brian was returning from Casper. It was almost like a salute. The timing was unbelievable.

ON THE DAY HE DIED, Ross was working in his position as controller at PineRidge Hospital. Ross had a deep respect for Lander's medical community. He thought it was a miracle that we had these wonderful facilities.

My wife Nancy and I have a little boy named Michael who came along about 10 years after our three older daughters. Frankly, I was worried that we were spoiling him rotten. Ross and I often talked about how this kid would turn out.

Ross would always reassure me. "Don't worry," he'd say. "The youngest, when they are this much younger than the rest of the family, will receive so much love from their parents and their older brothers and sisters, they will grow up very well adjusted. Then he'd point to himself and say, "By Golly, I'm living proof that the system works!"

I want to tell Ross's older brothers and his older sister Polly how much your little kid brother loved you. He said he had a great childhood and was smothered with love.

I hope during this eulogy that I haven't left anyone out. Ross always said that I wasn't very organized. One of his favorite jokes was to tell people about my "newspaper editor filing system."

It seems he didn't approve of me throwing everything into a file cabinet drawer and marking it: "Top of Desk, Oct. 23, 1984." He was too organized to imagine anyone filing things that way.

ON THE FRIDAY BEFORE HE DIED, Ross had completed one of the biggest deals of his life. It was a package we had been working on for months in South Dakota. He was able to finally pull off the whole deal in an hour and a half.

Afterwards, he called me from the Spearfish Racquetball club to give me the news. He was absolutely elated. He told me to take Nancy out to dinner to celebrate, which I did.

He said he almost jumped up and clicked his heels, he was so happy we'd finally put the deal together.

Ross concluded our phone conversation with a statement he often used, but this time one that I'll never forget:

"Billy Bob. Let me ask you. Do I do good work?"

Yes, Rosco, you sure do.

Stacy: A story of courage

"I'm not afraid to die. I feel like I faced death two years ago, but I came back, maybe to try to impart on a few people how precious life is. If I've done that, then I feel I've accomplished quite a lot."
— *Stacy Martell, May 31, 1989*

THE LANDER COMMUNITY lost a great friend Sunday when Stacy Martell died. He taught us all a lot about living and dying, life and death.

This frail young man had fought most of his life against Muscular Dystrophy. His struggle captivated his classmates and their parents. His courage was legendary. His understanding was immense. His patience with his situation made us stronger.

For years, he was a familiar sight in his motorized wheelchair, buzzing the neighborhoods of Lander. During one particular speedy trip, he rolled his chair and damaged his neck. Doctors told him he probably would never speak again.

Yet with patience and time, he figured out a way to talk. He talked well enough to address his graduating class in 1989, through an elaborate TV connection from his home on Bellvue to the high school fieldhouse.

The guest speaker that night played the song *Wind Beneath My Wings* as a tribute to Stacy. I was there. It was incredibly moving. There was hardly a dry eye in the place.

GRADUATIONS ARE EMOTIONAL EVENTS, anyway, but that one back in 1989 was almost totally unique.

It was unusual to find a class with this many all-stars. Top students like Joseph Gee and Cristy Hunt were exceptional, plus their supporting cast would have dominated other years' graduating classes. Teachers will attest to the outstanding nature of that year's class.

And it was an international group — with youngsters from Brazil, Denmark, Germany and Australia in the class — while others missed the ceremony because they were overseas.

But all this was overshadowed by a young man who couldn't even breathe on his own.

The graduation was Stacy Martell's night. That courageous young man had set a standard of bravery that none of his classmates could experience themselves. A lifetime victim of Muscular Dystrophy, he had struggled hard to live long enough to graduate.

And by his example, Stacy showed each of his classmates what real strength is.

This class was definitely special in the way its members treated its most severely handicapped member.

When he was a freshman, he wheeled his wheelchair to the library in order to skip the pep assembly. "There is always a crush of bodies, and it is a general hassle for me," he wrote in an essay he hoped to someday publish.

"This particular time, the vice-principal came and got me out of the computer room and told me I had to go. I was annoyed. This was going to cut into my computer time!

"When I got to the gym, I was asked to go out on the floor. The football team presented me with a football jersey and made me an honorary member of the team. I got a standing ovation from the student body. There was an incredible rush of emotion throughout the gym. It made me feel very special and well liked."

HE WROTE ABOUT HIS PHYSICAL DETERIORATION during a period in 1988 when he was hospitalized and had to be taken to Denver for specialized treatment:

"I felt I was really going downhill, and this affected me mentally also. I was depressed. I was going to turn 18 soon and all I could think of was my uncles who had MD and had died at ages of 17 and 18.

"At that point, I had accepted that my life was soon to end."

But Stacy bounced back. He got out of the hospital and learned to speak all over again, after being told by some doctors that he would never speak again.

He addressed his classmates at the 1989 graduation through the magic of video. And although he spoke haltingly at times, his voice was strong and his words were true to the point.

His personal writings reveal even more than his talk:

"There are times when I want desperately to be like everyone else. I've thought about marriage. There's a void when I think this won't happen, that I'll never be able to have a family of my own.

"But I know a person can't dwell on improbables. You have to take what you've got and go with it. I used to worry about what people thought of my body. But now I know that it's a person's inner self that's important, not your outer self. I've looked at my inner self: it's healthy, strong, vibrant, active. When I think of myself this way, I'm satisfied. I'm at peace with myself."

STACY MARTELL provided his classmates with insights that they could never have had without him.

They will go through the rest of their lives reaching out to handicapped people because they know it is not the "outer self that matters," but the "inner."

Stacy writes the following about death:

"I've lived, I've done my best, what happens, happens. I've seen an unspoken question in some people's eyes. It's 'Do you wish sometimes you had never been born?'

"Absolutely not! It hasn't always been easy, but I've met the challenges and I'm here to say that life is worth living."

Four

Workings
of an
Idle Mind

Experience is a hard teacher because
she gives the test first
and the lesson afterwards.
—*Vernon Law*

A slogan that fits Wyoming

⟫●⟪

Meanwhile, people are still "Finding Themselves In Wyoming" as record numbers of tourists come to our state.

⟫●⟪

"FIND YOURSELF IN WYOMING" had been used as a state tourism marketing slogan for the past six years. It had served the state well. Was it time for a new one?

In recent years, the state had used the promotional slogans "BIG Wyoming" and "Wyoming Is What America Was."

Before that, there were other slogans. Perhaps the two most common slogans used both formally and informally are "The Equality State" and "The Cowboy State," although these have rarely been used for tourism promotion.

All are fine. But is there a new slogan out there that better describes Wyoming?

Governor Mike Sullivan talks about the quality of Wyoming people. He likes to use the term "Last Best Place" in describing the state, which would be a fine slogan. Sullivan also likes to describe

Wyoming by saying, "The whole state is like one small community with unusually long streets."

Casper columnist Dave Kiffer (with his tongue planted firmly in his cheek) recently wrote a funny piece citing some different (bad) slogan ideas for Wyoming. Had an outsider made these claims, we would have been upset, but since they were made by a Wyomingite, we found them very funny. He offered slogans such as:

> "The Big Empty"
> "A Lasting Vacancy"
> "Wyoming: Don't Fall for the Rocky Mountain Lie"
> "Wyoming: Where You Can Look Farther
>   and See Less"
> "Wyoming: You Can't Get There From Here"
> "Wyoming Is What Wyoming Was"

THE LAST TIME A NEW PROMOTIONAL SLOGAN was generated for the state it was the line: "Wyoming: Where Nothing Stands In Your Way." It was planned as a slogan for the Department of Commerce to entice new industry to come to the state. It backfired under intense criticism and the old reliable "Find Yourself" was quickly substituted.

The Wyoming Division of Tourism went through the process of selecting its advertising agency recently. Part of that process included reviewing slogan ideas from candidates wanting to be the state's agency.

It might be important to note that other states have recently changed their slogans.

South Dakota came up with "Great Faces. Great Places." as a slogan. Montana was using "Unspoiled. Unforgettable." Meanwhile, people were still "Finding Themselves In Wyoming" as record numbers of tourists came to our state. Perhaps they were actually wandering around and ultimately found themselves here or perhaps the slogan has a more abstract meaning — come to Wyoming and find out who you really are!

My two favorite state slogans are those used by Texas: "It's Like A Whole Other Country" and British Columbia: "Super. Natural."

IN THE FINAL ANALYSIS, the state made the selection of a new slogan. And it is a mighty good one.

I was serving as a member of the Wyoming Travel Commission during this process. The people there were tireless in their efforts.

I'll never forget the hard work and good effort put in by the members of the commission during this period — people like Jim Hearne, Cheyenne; Pat Sweeney, Gillette; Clay James, Moran; Pam Rankin, Jackson; Rick Wilder and Bob Coe, Cody; Tim Rubald, Laramie; Kirk Kavanagh, Buffalo; Kathryn Baron, Sheridan; Gene Kupke, Lusk; Nancy Anselmi, Rock Springs; and Doris Ostrowski and Sue Bromley, Rawlins.

In my opinion, the Wyoming Travel Commission staff — which was headed by Gene Bryan with able assistance from Clyde Douglass, Wayne Wilkerson, Chuck Coon, Bill Lindstrom, Sherry Hughes, Carol Stearns, Linda Sauer, Jeff Olson and others — is the best in America.

THE NEW ADVERTISING AGENCY hired by the state Division of Tourism, Riddell Advertising of Jackson, came up with "Like No Place On Earth."

That slogan does a great job of describing the Wyoming I know.

Getting bombed

<hr>

Every 10 minutes, these awesome jets
would come thundering across Lander
Valley. They would come along the face
of Table Mountain, take a sharp turn
north toward my house,
come screaming along just
above the shingles and then disappear
over Crumps Mountain.

<hr>

BACK IN 1990, our newspaper ran a photo on the front page of an
FB-111 jet plane on a bombing run over the Lander area.

A great many people assumed that it was some sort of file photo,
as it was so clear and obviously snapped from close range.

Well, it wasn't a file photo. That guy flew right over my house.
You could wave at him. His eyes were blue. His hair was brown. He
didn't wave, but I could swear he nodded at me. And then he was
gone.

Every 10 minutes, these awesome jets would come thundering
across Lander Valley. They would come along the face of Table

Mountain, take a sharp turn north toward my house, come screaming along just above the shingles and then disappear over Crumps Mountain.

They were bombers from Ellsworth Air Force Base in Rapid City, and they were doing bombing runs over an "uninhabited" part of Wyoming.

Not only was I snapping photos of the jets coming over the house, but I always aimed my telephoto lens at the jet as it headed for the mountain, for I was convinced one of them would smash into it. Luckily for those pilots, I did not get that photo that day, not that I really wanted to.

WATCHING THOSE BOMBERS reminded me of one of the best speeches I have ever heard.

It was by former Astronaut Rusty Schweickart. It was at a symposium honoring Jacques Cousteau back in 1986, and he was talking about Cousteau's son, Phillipe, a famous advocate for world peace.

Schweickart, who earlier in his Air Force career was assigned to drop nuclear bombs on China, took Phillipe on a flight one day in an F-100. They ultimately ended up at a base with a simulator. Schweikart was able to get Phillipe a 30-minute stint flying an F-111 simulator.

Afterward, as Schweickart tells it, Phillipe was very, very quiet. Finally, he said, "You know, that was really fun. That was really fun."

Schweickart, who came to Lander in 1969 for the One Shot Antelope Hunt, used that story to point out how people can fall in love with technology. For that experience in the simulator was all about dropping bombs and shooting down enemy planes or attacking civilians. All of which involved killing lots of people.

He believes that somehow people need to maintain that love affair with technology yet somehow remove the war machine aspect from it. It often is not an easy task, he says.

And that day last month when the bombers and fighter-bombers were strafing my house, I admit to a total fascination with what those pilots were experiencing. Sure, it was scary, especially when you stopped to realize what those planes were capable of doing.

But it sure looked like fun, too.

Who am I?

Perhaps I am nothing
or I am something. Am I a spiritual
being having a human experience?
Or a human being dreaming about a
spiritual experience? Biologically,
I am the fruit of 800 generations.
Mentally, I don't know.

I AM THE PRODUCT of 800 generations of mankind.

Am I the sum of the parts, or am I a single being that has been transported through a jig-jag cycle of generations, from man to woman, throughout the years . . . recreated through the whims of chance . . . or of God? Or all the above?

I write this after midnight, which is quite normal for me. That is when I am most wistful, most full of curiosity about perplexing questions. Questions like:

What does all this mean?

What's going to happen to me?

Where did I come from?

And, who am I?

TRY AS I MIGHT I cannot recall thoughts that are not my own or at least thoughts that I think are my own. But are they really? Could they be the thoughts of another man who lived another time? Is that why I feel so good around the sea? My level of comfort is so high there that I can believe that I once was a Welshman or an Irishman.

I still am a product of those nationalities. I am Celtic. I look it and act it.

I also ponder the consequences of my life. Will my thoughts end when these bones and flesh and brain cells die? Or do they carry on in the deep recesses of someone else's mind, someone else yet to come? Will there be a person out there in the future who will carry my thoughts deep inside of them.

I doubt it, frankly.

THE BEST WAY FOR ME to send my thoughts into the future is through these words on this soon-to-be primitive computer. They are typed here simply and they will be read here simply.

I know not who will read them, but if they find them interesting, they can say they know something about Bill Sniffin.

It is early in the morning as I write this. I am at my most musing at these hours.

Perhaps the reason for my melancholy is that tomorrow I leave on a business trip with serious consequences. I hope and I pray that I will be successful in my efforts.

Unlike my ancestors, who worried about the fish or the weather, I am a businessman. There is a business deal out there that I need to conclude tomorrow and although it probably isn't quite as potentially life-threatening as those circumstances that confronted my ancestors, I no doubt worry about them in the same way. Perhaps many of them stewed into the night worrying about the outcome of the next day's events.

I KNOW FEAR TONIGHT. I worry about the future. I have always been so secure about myself. Self-doubting is not a normal state of mind for me. Yet I fear for the future in a security sense. I don't want to put myself or my family at risk, yet that is where I have put them.

Such a position makes me a fighter, but when I look at my family, I become ashamed because they may be disappointed.

My life has been one of continued success against great odds. And it shall be that way as long as I have strength in my muscles and a brain in my head. I am the hardest worker I know of and I shall continue to be this way.

I need to draw upon the strengths of my ancestors now.

Was I strong in those other lives? Did I roll over or run when confronted by adversity? If so, then I have a problem now. Somewhere in my past there have been some fighters. It is their genes that I am calling upon now. Make me strong. Carry me through. I need your perseverance and grit. Let us be champions. Let no man say that I — whoever I am — left the field of battle a defeated weakling.

THIS BODY I HAVE BEEN GIVEN is growing older and softer. It seems I have not taken too good care of it.

It was designed for lifting and pulling, I think. My short, stocky shape probably would have made for a good blacksmith or farmer. I certainly don't look like a king. Maybe I was a knight. Probably I was a foot soldier or the man who fired the cannons. Maybe I cleaned out the stables.

I need to get into shape. Perhaps it is not too late. Many people run in middle age and do very well. I need a distraction from all my work. Maybe such an activity should be running or at least walking. What did my ancestors do? They probably worked all the time . . . just like me.

THE SUM OF ALL THOSE PEOPLE IS ME. I just cannot recall anything from previous lives. I know that I have certain preordained traits such as liking bread and honey and mountains and feeding my insatiable mind. I just cannot absorb enough knowledge, which makes living in Lander a challenge and living my present lifestyle a curse. My idea of an intellectual evening is often watching a rented video. What a waste of my brain. Someday I may pay for this lack of responsibility.

WHO AM I? Perhaps I am nothing or I am something. Am I a spiritual being having a human experience? Or a human being dreaming about a spiritual experience? Biologically, I am the fruit of 800 generations. Mentally, I don't know.

What I do know is that I have the power to do some good on this planet. Maybe my present trials are part of a plan to make me strong. Steel does not get hard until you put it in the fire. And the hotter the fire, the harder the steel. I can certainly endure much more than my present challenges. I tire from the struggle, but I will not give up.

My ancestors won't let me. And neither will I.

(Note: The above was written during the mid-1980s when I was struggling with a major business transaction and a mid-life crisis. The death of my best friend, J. Ross Stotts, forced me to confront my own mortality. That resulted in my selling some of my properties in South Dakota and heading off to Great Britain to earn a master's degree. That trip yielded big dividends in that it showed me that the future was big in international travel, where much of my present-day business efforts are directed.

By the way, the deal that I was stewing about when I wrote this essay to myself turned out to be a big success.)

Give me
a morning
...like this morning

As I was taking all this in — my own
personal "painted morning,"
as I decided to call it — a rainbow
appeared off to the southwest
above Table Mountain. I thought myself
pretty lucky at that moment.

I WOULD LIKE TO SHARE a recent Wyoming morning with you.

This particular morning seemed extra special. For whatever reason, I woke up before sunrise. Our dog was barking and the wind was rustling the leaves outside our window.

I staggered out of bed. Feeling woozy and uncoordinated, I peeked out the window and saw some ominous clouds in the darkened sky. To those who know me, I'm a night person, a night owl who often will stay up past midnight. As a result, I don't like to get out of bed early in the morning, like on this particular morning.

Dressed in a sweatshirt, sweat pants and a pair of slippers, I walked outside to roll up the windows on the car. It felt like rain might be coming. There was lightning off to the east. In Wyoming, it is so dry that you can always tell impending rain by the smell of moisture in the air.

A gust of wind came up and pushed me against the car. I forced open the door and rolled up the windows.

As I started back to the house, I stopped and looked around. The sky was getting brighter, and it felt more like morning than night.

I SUPPOSE THERE ARE LOTS OF PEOPLE who get up every day at this hour. I envied them at this moment. It was beautiful in the outdoors. The experience was one that occurs so rarely to me, it was turning out to be a special morning.

The moon was shining in the west between two cloud banks, with Venus still visible at that hour. They were the only objects visible in the purple sky besides the clouds and an occasional lightning bolt.

I untangled the dog's rope. She was glad to see me and showed it by jumping and licking. I untied her and let her follow me around.

Off to the east, the sky suddenly was on fire. A gold ball had peeked over the hill. Dawn was arriving. The wind was dying down and the mountainsides turned golden with alpenglow — it was that time of day when the mountains reflect back the sun's early morning light.

It was raining in spots all around us, but the sky above me was clear. The view of the rising sun was breathtaking with gold, yellow and red colors mixing together.

Over the mountains, storm clouds still lingered with one, especially, jutting out above. It looked a lot like the Grand Teton in winter, all white and massive.

As I WAS TAKING ALL THIS IN — my own personal "painted morning," as I decided to call it — a rainbow appeared off to the southwest above Table Mountain. I thought myself pretty lucky at that moment.

I could hear cows mooing and sheep baaing down in the valley and a flustered wren scolding something off in the distance. Two magpies flew over my head making sounds like tiny horns honking. I thought I heard some music being played in the distance. Was that the high school band?

I had made a pot of coffee by then and was standing on the deck surveying the sights of my morning. As I looked toward my mountains, at my alpenglow, my thunderheads and my rainbow, I saw my shadow stretch out about 100 yards in front of me.

And I was glad that I had been up that morning to enjoy my very own "Wyoming Painted Morning." I hoped that others had been able to enjoy it, too.

Jewelry for noses?

Recently, two young women walked into the *Journal* and looked embarrassed. And they should have been. They had rings in their noses!

INADVERTENTLY TUNED IN to a music television show recently. I had been looking for either a good movie or a good basketball game. I got a music video instead.

There was one of my favorite songs being acted out on the screen by a guy with a ring in his nose. In his nose!

When you live in Wyoming, you probably miss out on some important national trends. I really had not realized that many of the major singers were putting rings in their noses.

This show, called "Night Tracks," is an MTV-type show, which apparently comes on late at night. It shows the same videos that MTV shows.

Now the overall quality of the video was a little risqué. Would I want my 12-year-old son to watch it? I think not. He watches DTV — also known as Disney TV, which uses something called Kids and Co. to do its videos. Much nicer.

Without getting too involved in the ongoing local debates over MTV, music lyrics and the overall message of many videos, this column shall confine itself to this strange nasal phenomenom.

This guy in the video was a fine-looking guy with a terrific voice. He even wrote the song. Why then did he have a ring in his nose?

I couldn't help wondering how that felt? It would seem like you would have this unreachable object in your nostril. It must be uncomfortable.

After that video finished, another came on. This time it was a young woman singing a popular song — and she had a ring in her nose, too. And her ring had two long chains connected to it that stretched around her head and around her neck. I couldn't help being distracted by this nose ring.

Now I'm tempted here to mention a ring that's been in my nose for about 27 years, but cowardice will prevent me from delving further into that subject.

RECENTLY, TWO YOUNG WOMEN walked into the *Journal,* and they looked embarrassed. And they should have been. They had rings in their noses! They kept giggling about it, and I finally asked them, "How does that feel?"

They laughed and said their nostrils were swollen, and, as a result, they could certainly feel them. "Why did you do that?" I inquired. They just giggled and ignored me as I was obviously way too old to understand.

Is this a new trend in Wyoming? I would hate to appear so old-fashioned and un-trendy. Maybe we all will soon be wearing nose rings.

If so, that nose-ring with the chains looked like it had a utilitarian purpose. You could always hang your car keys on the chain.

What goes around, comes around...

Well, it took 30 years,
but the sins of my youth
came home to roost early in the
morning last week.

THE SAYING THAT HEADS THIS ARTICLE is one of my favorites. As with many things, there seems to be so much truth in it. It is much like the Biblical saying, "As you sow, so shall you reap."

Well, it took 30 years, but the sins of my youth came home to roost (that's another one, by the way) early one morning.

Back in my younger days in the little town of Wadena, Iowa, I could be a mischievous brat. My hometown was a lot like Hudson. It was the same size and was located on a major road linking the two largest towns of our county.

And like Hudson, there was a major river running through the town.

One of the biggest events of my young life was the night the milk truck caved in the bridge. All of us kids ran down to see what the commotion was. The big truck had just made it across before the bed of the old bridge fell into the Volga River.

Later that summer, the new bridge was finally open. I can recall one night when one of my brothers and I thought up a neat trick. We took some of the old oil flares that marked piles of rubble next to the new bridge and put them in the middle of the road. This would stop traffic, we thought, and force people into making a short detour around the bridge.

Our devilish trick worked. We were hiding in the bushes giggling as several cars and trucks pulled up to the bridge, stopped, and then took the long way around.

WELL, I WAS WORKING LATE ONE EVENING and left the office at about 1 a.m.

At the intersection of Ninth and Fremont, there was a small cut in the new road construction where cars had been able to drive through. I had driven through there myself earlier in the evening on my way to work.

But not now. Three large safety barrels had been moved to block the road. I stopped and pondered my situation. No way could this be right. It must be a prank.

Finally, I decided to turn my car around and take the long way around.

And as I did that, I could almost swear I could hear the voices of some kids snickering in the bushes. It almost sounded like it may have come from a long time ago.

My home town

When I think of Wadena, Iowa,
vivid images come to mind.
I can see it in my memories.
I can smell it and I can feel it.

PICTURE THIS TINIEST OF TOWNS nestled in a valley with a lazy river running through it. Tree-covered hills surround this valley. There are a few fields along the valley bottom, but the most noticeable aspect of the environment is the abundance of trees.

This is a glacier-cut valley in an area of prairie Iowa that is not so flat. This town is about 18 miles west of the cliffs overlooking the huge Mississippi River. The valley is known as Little Switzerland.

Most times of the year, it is muggy in this valley. The moisture hangs in the air. And the smell of manure, usually pig manure, fills the air. You can drive by with your windows up with your air conditioner on, and you can still smell that farm odor, the smell of manure.

The manure is the ultimate recycling material. It serves as fertilizer, and the farmers in this valley, like most every other valley in the vast mid-American farmbelt, value it as wealth. With good manure, a farmer can improve his chances of a good crop by 20 percent. That is a good investment.

I can't tell you how many times I heard farmers smell the air and say that was the smell of money.

WADENA IN THE 1950s was a Saturday night town. We kids would head to the moviehouse on Saturday afternoons and watch a movie for a dime. That night, our parents would go "downtown" which involved mingling with what seemed like hundreds of people. People would just mill around and be sociable on those hot summer nights.

It's odd, but I distinctly recall dozens of men hanging out at Jim Crandall's barber shop on those nights. Jim was a famous ex-Marine and was some kind of war hero. He gave all the men buzz haircuts, which they still wore, military-style.

The bar, Johnny's Place, would be jumping, but we didn't go near it because my parents didn't drink. The smell of old beer oozing out from behind those mysterious doors amidst the smoke and the music and the loud carousing was always an attraction to my brothers and me.

Apparently, there was a lot of action at Johnny's Place that we young people were not aware of. Some years later, as local legend had it, the plumbing out back was plugged up. When the plumber went to free up the pipes, he found buckets full of used condoms. At least that was the story.

A general store was open on Saturday night. It was right next to Johnny's Place, so we could peer into the bar as we hung around the front of their store.

Jennings Hardware was on the same block. My best friend Neal Jennings would be there with his dad and two brothers.

We would headquarter at Grandpa Sniffin's little gas station and barber shop, which was located between Jennings and Johnny's. This allowed us to run free all over this one-and-only block of stores in downtown Wadena.

The little shop smelled of pipe smoke. Grandpa was never without a corncob pipe clenched in his teeth. He was a good old guy but not too talkative. I remember him letting us steer his old red pickup when he would drive the seven blocks from his and Grandma's house to the shop. They lived across the street from us and we spent lots of time there.

THE MOST COMMON FORM OF ATTIRE for the men was a pair of bib overalls and workshoes. Often, there would be a tee shirt or no shirt. Most of the men were big, husky fellows who seldom cleaned up. It was almost a badge of distinction to go to town "with the shit still on your shoes."

These men were war veterans. There were a few who didn't go to war, but most did. Even though World War II had ended 10 years earlier, talk of war and heroic times dominated the conversations.

The women talked about babies. Everywhere were babies. The entire country was experiencing a baby boom, even little Wadena, Iowa. The valley town was experiencing the biggest birthing boom in its history.

The town was home to 300 people and it consisted mainly of one Main street that was nine blocks long. The town ventured one block west and three blocks east. Smack in the center of town was the town park with a bandstand and a statue of a Civil War soldier in the middle of it.

The Volga River flowed through the south edge of town on a lazy trip from Fayette to the Mississippi. It provided a little fishing, a lot of ice skating and the infamous Bare Ass Beach, my favorite summer escape from the oppressive muggy heat.

Especially in the dog days in mid-August — we headed for the river. The trip was interesting in that we had to travel down the rows of corn field, through a nettle patch and across an abandoned railroad right-of-way and then we had to tiptoe among the leeches in the mud to get there.

I recently visited BAB with my young son, and it was not nearly so big nor so impressive as in my memories. I tried to envision those experiences when we little boys would splash around in the shallows while characters named "Fruit" and "Horse" would stand naked on the diving board and make obscene gestures. It was an unusual form of sex education, and it left an indelible impression.

Old BAB was a special place despite these diversions and perversions.

Picking the leeches (bloodsuckers) off our skin and from between our toes and under our armpits was always a hateful part of the swimming at BAB. But we had to do it. If we didn't, Mom would do it when we got home. By then, the leeches would be so full of blood it would really hurt, and Mom would threaten to not let us go back.

Some of my favorite jokes

During the course of a writing career that has spanned three decades and has included a series of public speaking appearances, it has been my good fortune to collect a number of my favorite stories. The three stories that are included here are my favorite stories to tell from the podium, either as a featured speaker or as an emcee.

My first speech: To a Sunday School class

One of the first times I was asked to speak to a group was shortly after I was first married. A local Sunday School teacher asked me to talk to her class of young girls about sex. I thought I could handle it, so I told her, "Yes, I would do that."

I went to mark it down on my desk calendar, and I wrote: "Talk to young girls at Sunday School about sex." Now after looking at that awhile, it seemed that didn't look right. So, I scratched out the word "sex" and penciled in "snowmobiling."

The next day, my wife came by my office, but I was out. She left some forms on my desk and noticed that I had written on my desk calendar that I was going to talk to the Sunday School class about snowmobiling.

Some time later, my wife met that Sunday School teacher while shopping. The Sunday School teacher had high praise for me. "Your husband did a wonderful job speaking to our girls last Sunday," she said.

"I can't imagine that he did such a good job," my wife told the teacher, "He's not very good at it. He's only done it twice.

"The first time he did it, he ran out of gas.

And the second time he did it, he fell off and hit his head on a rock."

A pig joke

A guy moved to the country and decided he wanted to be a small-time farmer. He went to an auction and bought 12 hogs. He loaded them up in his pickup and hauled them home.

Once home, he called his neighbor, an experienced hog farmer, and invited the guy over to check out his purchase.

The experienced farmer said they were good hogs, but there was just one problem. They were all female. But that was not such a big deal, the guy said. Just load them up in your pickup and bring them over to my yard. I have several boars and we'll get them bred. You really need to get your females bred this time of year. "Sure," the new farmer said.

The next morning, he loaded up the hogs in the back of his truck and hauled them over to the experienced farmer's lot. He unloaded them and waited all day. Then he brought them home. Before leaving, he asked the experienced farmer, "How will I know if they were successfully bred or not?"

"If they were bred successfully, tomorrow morning, your hogs should be grazing," the experienced farmer replied.

Well, the next morning, the new farmer got up early and looked out the window. The hogs were not grazing. So he loaded them up and took them over to the experienced farmer's lot again.

Again, the next morning, the hogs were not grazing.

He hauled them over the next day, too, in his pickup. Still no luck. This went on for more than a week.

Finally, the day after hauling the hogs back home from his neighbor's place, he awoke the next morning and turned to his wife. He said, "I can't bear the disappointment. Would you look out the window and see if those hogs are grazing?"

"Yes, dear," she replied.

After a few moments, he hollered at his wife, "Well? Are they grazing? Tell me what they are doing."

His wife paused and then said, "I don't know how to tell you this.

"They definitely are not grazing.

"But 11 of them are sitting in the back of the pickup, and the 12th one is in the driver's seat honking the horn."

The bell ringer

A priest ran an ad seeking a new bell-ringer. His old one had retired, and he was interviewing applicants. A man appeared who had two broken arms. He said he wanted the job of the bell ringer. The priest asked how could he do that? He couldn't use his arms.

The man said he was Irish and had a very strong head, and he wanted to show the priest how he could do it. Together they climbed up the bell tower. Once on top, the man lowered his head and ran headlong into the bell, and it let out a wonderful peal — it was the best the priest had ever heard. "I'm very impressed," the priest said. "Could I see you do that again?"

The man said, "Sure." He lowered his head and started running toward the bell. But after the first time he had done it, the bell had started swinging back and forth. The man missed the bell and went flying right over the side and fell down.

The priest looked down in horror. There was the man, lying on the ground, with a crowd quickly gathering around him. The priest hurried down the stairs and went outside to where the crowd had gathered.

A policeman was there. He asked, "Does anyone know this man?"

The priest spoke up. "I don't know his name. But his face rings a bell."

Five

Journal-ism

What we want, and what we shall have,
is the royal American privilege
of living and dying in a country town,
running a country newspaper,
saying what we please when we please,
how we please and to whom we please.
—*William Allen White*
Emporia (Kansas) Gazette, 1911

Evolution of an editor

The go-go had gone-gone.
There was movement in property
values, all right, but straight down.
One bumper sticker read,
"Lord, please give me one more boom.
This time, I promise not to piss it away."

THE WORST EXPRESSION I could think of to describe the worst editor I knew was that he was a blind booster.

Blind Boosterism — that damn the torpedoes, full speed ahead, put on the blinders, pollyanna-type of editor who served as a town's cheerleader and full-time promoter.

Not me. I was a skeptical kind of editor. You know those guys. Sort of like Ben Bradlee of the *Washington Post*. Or, in earlier times, like William Allen White. You know, an editor who called a spade a spade and even embarrassed the emperor when he told him he had no clothes on.

But ultimately I seem to have changed, and I must confess that I have occasionally become a proponent of, uh, geez, it is so hard to come out and say it, but, "blind boosterism!" Yes, that dreaded expression.

This is coming from an editor who has won the National Herrick Editorial Award and earned a first prize in investigative reporting from the National Newspaper Association. Pretty impressive stuff. Not the sort of prizes they give to editors who are blind boosters in their towns.

So what made me change?

I F THERE WAS A TURNING POINT, it occurred somewhere around 1982. Wyoming had been in a tremendous growth cycle. Population had grown from 300,000 to almost 500,000 in 12 short years. Times were good. Wyoming people were known as the Arabs of the West. If we were a nation, we would have been the eighth largest coal producing country on the planet. And we were awash in oil and uranium.

And in a world that craved energy, we thought we had it made. While the East shivered and the Midwest closed their plants, Wyoming was booming. "Let the bastards freeze" was boldly emblazoned on one bumper sticker displayed at the time.

D URING THAT 12-YEAR BOOM PERIOD, I had taken over the semi-weekly *Wyoming State Journal* in 1970 and immediately made a name for myself. I won the top editorial writing award in Wyoming three times in that decade.

It was a very rewarding time for a hard-hitting, crusading editor. We blasted the school district for all of its mistakes, and a superintendent resigned as a result. Our coverage probably prevented a mayor from winning an election. We completely changed a police department in a neighboring small town — and got nominated for the Pulitzer Prize for that work.

Our paper got into angry inter-city editorial battles with a neighboring town, Riverton. We battled over college, hospital, airport and highway issues. Editorials spewed forth from my typewriter, full of outrage, disappointment, calls for change and occasionally even ridicule. Nobody could call me a booster, by God.

We cautioned developers, and we questioned environmentalists. All politicians were fair game. We made some enemies and a lot of friends. It was important to be writing these kinds of editorials during these heady growth years. Times were good and these important messages needed to be stated.

To paraphrase the famous editor, H. L. Mencken, we "afflicted" many of "the comfortable."

▌T SEEMED TO ME that in a go-go, fast-growing, get-rich-quick environment, such editorials served a great purpose. They often served as a conscience for the community. They served as a restraint to keep things from getting out of control. They were sort of a reminder that there are often two sides to each issue and let's not be too hasty.

But in 1982, things changed. Suddenly there were no more markets for uranium. A huge U.S. Steel iron ore mine closed that destroyed 41 percent of the local economy. Some 2,000 jobs were lost in the mine closures. Oil prices plummeted, jolting the state.

Wyoming had more than $3 billion in the bank, thanks to forward thinking during those heady years. This money was from severance taxes. But suddenly, the money fountain turned into a money pit. There wasn't enough money to provide the services to which the people of Wyoming had become accustomed.

And in my town, things were, in a word, terrible.

A major bank closed and that led to over 28 key businesses closing their doors. Our main downtown block of stores was three-fourths empty. People were moving out or declaring bankruptcy. Four of my top 10 advertisers were out of business.

Our J.C. Penney Store closed after almost 50 years. The first Penney Store was in Kemmerer, Wyoming, and our local store was one of the early ones. The owner of the building finally rented it out — to a professional whittler. Can you imagine that? From a J.C. Penney Store to a whittler?

People were discouraged. I was sick at heart. It was not fun writing blistering editorials anymore.

The go-go had gone-gone. There was movement in property values, all right, straight down. One bumper sticker read, "Lord, please give me one more boom. This time, I promise not to piss it away."

About the most nasty editorial I could write was when the chairman of U. S. Steel, David Roderick, was quoted as saying, "We aren't in the business of making steel. We are in the business of making money." And what he didn't say is, *and by the way, to hell with Lander, Wyoming, wherever that is.*

▌HE OTHER HALF OF MENCKEN'S FAMOUS LINE about afflicting the comfortable was "and comfort the afflicted." And I think that is when I quit being such an aggressive editorial writer.

Suddenly, I was writing about how nice it was just to get to live in Wyoming. I wrote about our mountains and our wildlife. And how in just eight minutes, you could be standing in a two-million acre national forest. I reminded people that when they got there, they were welcome on "my spread" and it was theirs, too. And it was free.

I wrote editorials about how we had to work together and diversify our economy. I used the quote "Tough times quit. Tough people don't." And I reminded them of the old western saying that "a wishbone is no substitute for a backbone."

PEOPLE WOULD COME UP TO ME and thank me for things I wrote. "You really reminded me why we still live in this place," they would say, as if to remind them, that they could always move away to Denver or California or the Nevada gold mines.

I wrote about how the cost of living had gone down and that we needed to be more prudent. And how we also needed to shop at home.

Once I wrote a timely editorial reminding people that now was when the great fortunes of the 21st century were going to be made around Lander.

Prices were so low, and there was so much property for sale at sacrifice prices, I predicted that people who made those purchases now would be the ones who would be rich later.

Many people believed me and went out and bought real estate, which by my figuring, would help everybody. I figured once the housing glut was eliminated, all real estate would go up in price, which would be good for everyone who owned homes, anyway. And it worked.

NOW THINGS ARE HEALING. The bust is over.

Our community has adjusted to this new type of environment. People are upbeat and they have many projects in the works. It feels good around here. Housing prices are up. There is no longer a glut of underpriced homes on the market. Our downtown is filling back up. Credit is loosening.

And we occasionally are even starting to squabble with Riverton again on small items.

And me? Well, I'm tired of being a blind booster. I think I'm going to raise a little hell one of these days on my editorial page. And I'm looking forward to it.

Investigative reporting #101

≫•⊙•≪

We don't have cynics working at my newspaper. And I am not a cynic either. I happen to think the world is a pretty good place. Life has been very good to me and although I am considered a competent reporter, I don't believe you have to think the whole world stinks in order to be a good investigative reporter.

≫•⊙•≪

(Note: The following is my first guest lecture, given in 1986, to students at the Centre for Journalism Studies at Cardiff, Wales. The talk discusses some reporting experiences that occurred in Wyoming.)

IBRING YOU GREETINGS FROM AMERICA. Our journalists have a curiosity of how this wonderful business of ours is accomplished here.

Forgive me as I go along here if it appears that I misuse your

English language. As George Bernard Shaw once said, "Britain and America are two countries divided by a common language."

One reporter I know, who worked for awhile on a British newspaper, claimed that less than two-thirds of the words we both use are interchangeable.

With that in mind, please stop me if I proceed on a subject and give you an unclear impression. Above all, and especially in this business, let's proceed with clarity.

And if I talk about editing, which I understand you call subbing; or if I talk about a jump, which you call a turn; or a sidebar, which you call a tagline; well…bear with me. I'm not familiar with many of your terms and the ones I've just named came from a conversation I had with a reporter who worked for a Surrey newspaper.

I might also share with you my enthusiasm for coming home to my ancestry. Three-fourths of my roots come from the British Isles.

The name Sniffin comes from my father's side, which is the name given to people who hail from Kniveton over in Derby County. These people were originally called Kniffens, but problems with being able to read the spelling of the names caused some of us to ultimately be named Sniffin, thus my name. Perhaps this is an ideal name for a journalist who specializes in investigative reporting, but it came about purely as an accident of birth.

On my father's other side is a family named Flanagan, which of course is Irish.

My mother's parents provided my most direct link to Cardiff. My grandmother on that side was named Jones and came to America from Wales. My wife Nancy denies that I bear any resemblance to the singer Tom Jones, however.

On my mother's other side is a grandfather named Brockmeyer, a good German. That influence, no doubt, keeps the other parts inside of me organized.

ALSO BEFORE GETTING INTO MY SUBJECT, I might also talk briefly about a project that's dear to my heart. I am one of the candidates for the Journalist in Space program sponsored by NASA.

In spite of the terrible accident that killed seven astronauts, including a school teacher, I am still planning on going on that trip if lucky enough to be selected.

But, I am here to talk to you today about investigative reporting on community newspapers.

In America, we usually define a community newspaper as a non-daily and usually in a community under 10,000 population. These rules of thumb are not hard and fast, however. But for this discussion, let's use this as a way to describe this type of newspapering.

And perhaps we can use my newspaper as a typical example. Here are some facts about the *Wyoming State Journal* in Lander, Wyoming, USA:

1. It serves a community of about 7,000 people. It's surrounded by desert and huge mountains so there is very little rural population. The entire area served by our newspaper would barely include 20,000 people. This mountainous country is close to Yellowstone National Park. There are nearly 40 places over 13,000 feet high in our county.

2. The paper is published twice weekly, on Monday and Wednesday.

3. The news in it is totally local. Little regional or national news is published. Regional and national daily newspapers provide this news service.

4. Our news department consists of an editor-publisher (me), a news editor, a sports editor and a feature editor. There are 20 other employees in advertising, composition, circulation, business and press departments.

5. Circulation is 4,000.

6. A typical Monday paper is 16 broadsheet pages with the Wednesday paper about 20 broadsheet pages for a total of 36 pages per week.

7. The newspaper is highly automated. We use a high-speed offset press that can print 14,000, 12-page broadsheet papers per hour.

8. We don't use any hot lead. It is all offset printing. Type is set by the reporters directly into personal computers.

9. We have no unions represented in our plant. We feel we pay fair wages and offer good benefits.

I think I have the best job in the world. And as I look out here at you master's candidates, I can predict that at some time in your career you will long to get back to having a job similar to mine.

Many of the great editors and publishers in America have grown tired of the big city life and long to get back to their roots in the small towns of America. I would expect that many of you at some time in your futures may become involved again in community journalism.

In America, big-time editors like Ben Bradlee of the *Washington Post* and NBC-TV anchorman Tom Brokaw own community newspapers and radio stations around the country in communities the same size as mine.

Now that I've established that my job is the best in the world...how does a small newspaper like this do investigative reporting?

WE HAVE BEEN QUITE AGGRESSIVE over the years in our reporting. Our readers and our news sources know this. I believe in our business you "get what you give." Thus, our readers and our news sources know we do this type of reporting. We are constantly receiving tips — most of which are anonymous. It's not unusual for us to receive secret material that's been put in an unmarked envelope and slipped under our front door in the middle of the night!

I define investigative reporting as reporting a story that you normally wouldn't get with conventional reporting. It involves much extra work. It can also involve some personal risk. In our country, the majority of our investigative reporting efforts are related to government.

Our paper has been recognized nationally with major awards for two investigative pieces over the last 11 years. We have won many lesser awards, but I will discuss for you the two that won major awards.

I might also emphasize my personal philosophy, which is that there are too many cynical people in our business in the United States. Shortly after Watergate brought down the Nixon presidency, it seemed like many newspapers, large or small in my country were looking under every rock and digging up much dirt. Most of this was justified in the name of "investigative reporting."

We don't have cynics working at my newspaper. And I am not a cynic either. I happen to think the world is a pretty good place. Life has been very good to me and although I am considered a competent reporter, I don't believe you have to think the whole world stinks in order to be a good investigative reporter.

Today I'm going to tell you about two instances of investigative reporting at a community newspaper in Wyoming.

In one case, we won first place in the National Newspaper Association contest for investigative reporting. It involved abuses by a police department in a small neighboring town where the citizens endorsed Gestapo-type tactics by its local police in an effort to drive a segment of their population out of town because they thought they were hippies. This effort was nominated for a Pulitzer Prize.

Another series of stories involved a cover-up by our local public high school. The school annually gave students standardized tests that measured what they were learning against test results from schools all across the country.

That series won many awards and sparked a considerable amount of similar articles in other newspapers on their schools' testing results.

And I should hasten to add here that most of the information we were able to develop was public record under the laws of our country. You just had to know where to look and to whom to ask the right questions.

Law and order come to Dubois

Our community of Lander is the county seat of Fremont County, an area that is larger than seven of the states in our country. It is a huge area.

Fremont County stretches over 120 miles from one corner to the other. This is almost the same distance as from London to Cardiff.

In the far northwest corner of our county is the little town of Dubois. It has a population of about 1,000 people and sits in a beautiful spot atop Togwotee Mountain Pass, which leads to Jackson Hole and Yellowstone Park, Wyoming.

An unusual situation occurred in this community in the summer of 1977, yet it wasn't that unusual throughout America. There was a generation gap.

Because there were no jobs, the younger generation of Dubois had moved away. They moved to Colorado or California or even Jackson. For all practical purposes this generation was absent from the community.

But another group of young people of the same generation moved in. These were hippie types, as they were known back in the late 1970s. They dressed strangely. Men wore their hair long; women wore flowing colorful dresses and sandals. They smoked marijuana and were flagrant about their individualist lifestyles.

Dubois, Wyoming is a cowboy place. People there often wear their hair short, wear cowboy boots and Levis and use beer and whiskey as their drugs of choice. Many of them didn't trust liberals and felt these newcomers were unpatriotic in their opposition to the Vietnam War. They were also frightened that these newcomers were having a negative effect on their young people who were still in their community attending schools.

Our newspaper had a prize-winning correspondent and columnist (Cynthia Boyhan) who lived in Dubois. She felt the town council there had adopted a policy of harassment against these newcomers. She felt these people's civil rights were being violated by the town's small police department at the request of the town council and the mayor.

That reporter and I held a meeting on the situation and decided to go ahead and investigate it. We arrived at the conclusion that even though the majority of citizens of Dubois apparently agreed with its town government's philosophy, it still was a violation of these people's civil rights under the American constitution.

We decided to use the same system used by the *Washington Post* in its Watergate coverage when it came to doing the story. Unless we were there or heard the comment ourselves, there would need to be a third party corroborating every incriminating statement.

There were many charges of secret deals; of a town judge allegedly abusing his powers; of a police officer allegedly offering to reduce charges in exchange for a weekend in bed with one of the young females involved; and charges of police brutality against these people.

The articles were published in a five-part series accompanied by editorials, columns, photos and editorial cartoons. There were many letters to the editor from people in the various communities in our service area — the majority of which were supportive of the local police and critical of our stories. Yet, we plowed ahead.

In the end, the local judge was rebuked. The policeman most responsible for the crackdown quit the force and took off. And trumped-up charges against eight of the young people were ultimately dismissed. A state investigation was planned, but by the time it was conducted, things had settled down and most of the principles had left town or left their jobs.

People in Dubois quietly went about their business. Some of them still didn't understand why we did our stories. We received tremendous amounts of praise by our peers. The series of articles was being acclaimed as the best piece of investigative reporting done in Wyoming in recent memory.

I, for one, was left feeling frustrated that we hadn't been able to finish the job adequately. Although we had obviously accomplished a great deal, much that we thought we were going to do wasn't done. I was deeply disappointed by the fact that our limited resources resulted in us not doing as complete a job as I thought we were going to do.

We hadn't proved that an officer had really propositioned the young girl because her roommate who had told us she overheard the conversation disappeared on a hitch-hiking trip to Florida and was never heard from again.

The judge somehow managed to misplace records that we thought showed he had allegedly misused his power — a crime that could have sent him to jail. I felt the local county attorney stalled and dragged his feet after telling us he would help us investigate the situation. The state promised an investigation but stalled so long that it seemed irrelevant, finally.

And we were left with a situation where many of our readers really didn't understand why we went after the story so hard in the first place...

In the final analysis, we found that much good was accomplished. Young people had been threatened with jail when they didn't deserve it. A town had been polarized and guns were being waved around as a way to solve problems. Our articles seemed to cool down these heated confrontations.

Townspeople in Dubois ultimately quit harassing the newcomers. Winter soon came and many of them headed back to Florida.

And today, the subject rarely comes up concerning the time when "law and order" came to Dubois.

The School Testing Fiasco

We stumbled onto this story accidentally.

It concerns an exposé we published on our high school in which it was determined that students were scoring in the bottom one-fourth of students from all across our country in standardized testing. A high school in our country usually consists of four grades, freshmen to senior, with students ranging in age from 13 to 18.

What made this unusual was that our school had a good reputation. And we all took pride in the education that our public school was providing our young people.

Certainly the school didn't lack for tax dollars being spent on providing that education. Lander has always been well-known throughout the state for the high salaries paid to teachers. The school also has some of the newest facilities of any school district in the state.

We had a daughter who was a freshman in the high school at the time. When she brought home the results of her test, I wondered aloud to my wife how well the school, as a whole, did in comparison to the schools across the state and across the country?

When I inquired at the superintendent's office, I was rebuffed. Not only did he refuse to give me the results, but he was obstinate in the way he evaded my questions.

By now, my nose for news was starting to react. Had they just stalled me or given me some other plausible excuse such as "the results were not ready," I might have just let the matter drop. But they showed me there was something wrong by the way they reacted.

Later that night, I received an anonymous phone call. It was from someone at the school. He confirmed for me that something was terribly wrong. I had suspected the test scores must have been around the 50 percentile mark, which would have made the school only "average" when compared with other schools around the country. This person assured me it was worse than that.

The next day, I called the school and told the guidance department I was coming up there and I wanted the test scores. They told me they couldn't give them to me. But I said I was coming up anyway.

Meanwhile, I called our newspaper's attorney and alerted him that I may need a court order to get the information, as I knew it was public record. In America, only personal and personnel records are confidential.

When I got to the school, I confronted the administrators responsible for the testing and asked for the results. They said they couldn't provide me with this information. I told them that I would have to call my lawyer and get a court order. They then said they would contact the superintendent and get back to me. I told them I would wait there. They returned to the room and told me they would give me the results that afternoon, which they did.

The test scores were devastating. They showed our high school students testing in the lower one-fourth of all students across the country.

Our series of stories stunned the community. In one memorable confrontation at the local Rotary Club, the school superintendent tried to defend the test scores by attacking me. At the end of his talk, he threw up his hands, and stated loudly, "I know you can't win an argument with a man who buys ink by the barrel. They have the power of the press, you know."

I didn't say anything in response to that statement at the time, but later I wrote a column titled "The Power of Information versus the Power of the Press." In it I tried to explain that we weren't abusing any of our powers — we merely were informing the public, which is our job, with information that we felt they needed to know.

In the aftermath of all this, the school district made some drastic changes. The school board, which is an elected body that oversees the schools, encouraged the schools' superintendent to leave, added counselors and hired a curriculum director. They also initiated a study of the district which resulted in a gradual increase in credits needed to graduate from 18 to 24. They also closed up what was formerly an open campus situation, which had students wandering away from school throughout the day.

In summary:

These two examples show how a reporter can get involved in investigative reporting even though the newspaper isn't large.

A good aspect of such reporting is the intimate knowledge one gets from getting that involved in a story. You know your news sources well and you also get a tremendous satisfaction out of the good that your story accomplishes.

A negative aspect is that you often come under a large share of criticism. And you aren't as immune from it as you would be on a larger paper. There have even been cases where reporters were physically abused for stories they've done. Often your readers in small communities don't understand why you seek out this "bad news" to write about.

In summary, though, I must say that some of the most rewarding work I've ever done in this business was in investigative reporting.

You can sleep well at night knowing that what you did actually helped your community.

Teen editors show savvy

They didn't run away from the topic that was gripping their school; they confronted it like good editors. Upon further questioning by me, it was obvious these kids did their homework.

T ODAY'S TEENAGE JOURNALISTS are not timid.

I found that out while discussing investigative reporting with about 30 Wyoming school newspaper editors one Monday in 1992 in Casper. They were there for the annual Wyoming High School Press convention.

These young people listened to many speakers, participated on many panels and discussed what they could do to better serve their schools.

I suggested they do stories about test scores. And school budgets are important, I told them, since students are the ultimate consumer of what a school is selling.

We didn't talk about topics like teen sex, suicide, abortion and sexually transmitted diseases.

Or, I should say, I didn't talk about those topics. When we went around the room to see what kinds of stories these students were tackling, the result would have made most Wyoming editors envious of these teen editors' guts.

An editor from Gillette said her staff did in-depth stories about suicide after two students killed themselves during the school year. They didn't run away from the topic that was gripping their school; they confronted it like good editors. Upon further questioning by me, it was obvious these kids did their homework. Their work wasn't reckless and it wasn't irresponsible. They worked with authorities to make sure their messages were accurate and conducive to improve the situation among their student population.

TWO FEMALE SCHOOL EDITORS from Douglas described a survey they compiled in their school last year where every student was quizzed anonymously about teen sexual habits. Their results scared them and they responded by publishing information on how to avoid STDs (sexually transmitted diseases).

An editor from Buffalo described efforts in her school where they worked against teen drinking and driving. They asked tough questions of their classmates and they reported fairly.

In Riverton, the editors had already tackled just about every story idea I could think of, and the school year wasn't one-fourth over.

An editor from Cheyenne was interested in rating teachers, as a way of improving their overall education effort.

Down in Rock Springs, the teenage editors contended all last year with an ongoing controversy over the question of abortion.

OVERALL, THE YOUNG PEOPLE WERE IMPRESSIVE. The press group was headed by Dubois Journalism teacher Susan Kinneman, who also happens to be my kid sister.

She is the advisor for the national-award-winning *Ram Pages* high school paper at Dubois. She deserves a lot of credit for organizing one heck of a meeting.

Journal a national leader in the use of computers

It is funny is see how visitors to the
Journal peer around looking for
those clanking, creaking old linotype
machines that provided
the highlight of their last tour,
probably some 20 years ago.

IF THE *JOURNAL* IS ANY REFLECTION, it can be argued that we have, indeed, moved into the computer age.

Our staff uses a total of 16 computers. We have another four computers in storage, one in Dubois, one at my home and one on loan to a newspaper in South Dakota. This brings the grand total to 23 computers. This is for a newspaper that has 18 full-time equivilent employees. The computers are also used by the *Wind River News* and by Rocky Mountain International, a company that operates out of our building.

When people visit the *Journal*, they often are astonished at the number of computers being used. We use them for news writing, ad building, circulation billing and bookkeeping. Some of them are networked, and some work independently. Two of them are lap-top computers that can be used with four AA batteries and allow writers to type their stories anywhere, from a car seat to a gym bleacher to a courthouse office to an airline seat.

It is funny is see how visitors to the *Journal* peer around looking for those clanking, creaking old linotype machines that provided the highlight of their last tour, probably some 20 years ago. Although our modern computers do vastly more than those old linotypes, they aren't nearly so impressive.

Those old machines used melted lead and they spitted and snorted and blew off steam. A rancid odor hung around the machine, and the people who operated them often weren't very nice. You wouldn't be very nice, either, if you had to sit in front of one of those beasts all day.

BUT BACK TO THE PRESENT. Few people are aware that the *Journal* was an international leader in the use of such computers. We installed our first Apple Macintosh in the spring of 1985. We could not find a newspaper our size anywhere that was using this technology. We wrote the book on how to use what has come to be known as "desktop publishing" in the newspaper industry.

Today, more than 4,000 newspapers in America use this technology. When we started, there were probably fewer than 10, and certainly none within 1,000 miles.

This computerized miracle of news writing technology is the third wave to come along in my 29-year career. I started in that era of hot lead and loud, banging linotypes.

In the mid-1960s, photo-typesetting machines came along and replaced the hot-lead machines forever. And nobody misses that era, either.

The new machines were costly and involved an expensive process where photographic paper was used to create galleys, which are stories in a long narrow column. The new machines dove-tailed with the advent of offset printing, which provided faster, cleaner printing and much better reproduction of ads and photos. In 1969, we installed an offset press that today has a 12-page capacity.

That second wave lasted 20 years and now, through the invention of lasers, direct printing onto paper was born. That was the secret of our move to desktop publishing in 1985. We could now print our galleys directly on plain bond paper and eliminate the costly photographic paper.

I recall telling my fellow Wyoming publishers at the 1986 State Press Association convention that we were switching to this new technology. Not one of them had even heard of it. Today, they all are using it.

We use mainly Apple Macintosh computers and Apple laser printers. We have Apple and Tandy portables and a an IBM for bookkeeping.

IN THE MEANTIME, some folks think we have become experts at computers. I was invited to speak at several national computer shows about our experiences out here on the frontier.

The people in the audience were always amazed that we could accomplish something like that out here in such a remote area.

But none of us were really geniuses who had the ability to look into the future. Frankly, the reason we switched to this technology was that in 1985, the economy in Lander was so bad, we couldn't afford those expensive photographic typsetters. We had to figure out a cheap way to produce our galleys. Sometimes necessity is, indeed, the mother of invention. And in this instance, it also turned the *Journal* into a national pacesetter.

Book forewords
for comic poet
Bill Jones

It is not unusual for him to ride off
on his old nag with his beat-up old hat
at an angle, and just when he turns and
winks at you, his horse stumbles and
down Bill goes in a cloud of dust.

WYOMING'S FUNNIEST PERSON is Cowboy Poet Bill Jones. He is a
good friend and long-time columnist for the *Wyoming State Journal*.

I was flattered a few years ago when Bill asked me to write the
foreword for his new book *Dudes From Hell*.

Now writing a foreword for a book is a serious business. I
ground out a perfectly adequate foreword that properly recognized
Bill for his good works.

In a flight of whimsy, though, I also wrote a funny, off-the-wall
foreword that he could hopefully get a laugh from, and then throw
away.

In typical Bill Jones fashion, though, he printed both in his book.
I present them both here. Which do you like the best?

A Foreword:

IT IS EASY TO LIKE BILL JONES.

This transplanted Easterner has brought good feelings to thousands of people in the West with his down-home style of cowboy humor.

Bill Jones has been writing a column for our *Wyoming State Journal* for some time now. Our readers constantly tell me how much they enjoy his unique brand of humor. Much of what you will be reading in his book was originally published in our newspaper.

There are many cowboy poets around. And I am sure that Bill feels the highest compliment he can get is to be called a "cowboy poet."

But I see him as more than that. He is truly a western humorist, much in the same vein as a Will Rogers or a Mark Twain.

He was named Wyoming's funniest person in a comedy joke-off in 1991, defeating finalists from Laramie and Riverton. The crowd gave him a standing ovation at the end for his brand of clean, funny material.

Bill Jones is one of the best storytellers around. His sense of timing, the variety of his subjects and his appreciation for the audience he is talking to indicate this guy is going to go far.

Not only is he an outstanding poet, but he can pick on a guitar, sing a little, tell outrageous stories and write a terrific column. With his multitude of talents, he will go far.

It won't be long before we all will be proud to say, "I knew Bill Jones back when he was a cowboy poet in Lander, Wyoming."

I believe this book proves he is just now doing his best work. Hold on to your hats. It's going to be a great ride watching this funny man's career soar.

Here is my alternative version:

BILL JONES IS A MAN OF FEW WORDS. By that, I mean he doesn't know many words.

He is a legend in his own mind. He is a modest man, but then he has a lot to be modest about. He rode out of the East looking for a place where the roads end and the trails begin.

He told me, "This isn't the end of the world, but you can almost see it from here."

He has been writing a column for our newspaper, the *Wyoming State Journal,* for some time now. As a journalist, he is learning to separate the wheat from the chaff. Unfortunately, he usually prints the chaff.

A well-known reader once said this about a newspaper columnist: "He should have a pimp for a brother so that he would have someone to look up to." But enough kind words for this funny man.

As the head cowboy at a dude ranch, he can pretend to be pretty hot stuff. I've seen Jack Palance, and this is no Jack Palance. Maybe Jack Benny, but not Jack Palance.

It is not unusual for him to ride off on his old nag with his beat-up old hat at an angle and just when he turns and winks at you, his horse stumbles and down Bill goes in a cloud of dust.

As his horse trots off, Bill gets up and brushes himself off. He makes quite a sight, standing there alone in the middle of the pasture. It is at times like that that Bill can best be described as "a man out standing in his field."

Six

The Outdoors

All is perspective.
To the worm, digging in the ground
is more relaxing than going fishing.
—*Clyde Abel*

Ram-ming around mountaintops

You spend hours and hours scanning the mountain…Your eyes get bleary and your neck gets stiff. You look and look. Then you look some more…You look everywhere, always hoping…

DOES THIS SOUND LIKE FUN?
- Running up and down the summit of a 12,000 foot mountain.
- Leaning into a gale wind of 50 m.p.h..
- And getting snowed on during the first day of September.
- All the above at the same time.

It was.

That's some of the essence of Rocky Mountain bighorn sheep hunting in Wyoming.

I drew a sheep permit this year and spent much of the first week of September in the Absaroka Mountains looking for rams. We spent plenty of time hunting with no time shooting. We just didn't see any rams.

My guide, Dan Kinneman of Dubois, who is also my brother-in-law, originally asked to remain anonymous until I got a ram. He was baffled by the lack of qualifying sheep in this particular place in Area 5. He had guided hunts into this area for 16 years and never before had he been skunked when it came to even seeing a ram.

An unusual aspect of our hunt was that there were four other hunting parties in the immediate vicinity. This also was rare. Perhaps these guides had been in the area earlier and spooked the rams? I speculated. I don't know how successful they were.

We started our hunt at 4 a.m. on opening day. As we rode our horses up some switchbacks under the pale light of the moon, my guide was telling me what to do if we encountered a grizzly. There had been a lot of grizzly dung around our camp and one of the neighboring guides had had his camp destroyed several times by bears. We were in bear country and I was nervous.

"So, tell me again about what we should do if we encounter a grizzly?" I asked.

"Well, you've got to get off your horse."

"But that doesn't make sense," I offered. "This horse is my only way to get away from a grizzly."

"On the contrary. Your horse could dive head-long down the mountain. You might have seen cowboys ride that way in the movie *The Man From Snowy River,* but believe me, you won't survive a trip like that if you were to attempt it. If you see a bear, get off your horse!"

"Okay. okay."

WE RODE ON IN THE DARKNESS. Besides the adrenaline pumping through my body due to my first sheep hunt, the added potential of a grizzly bear encounter really made my hair stand on end.

As we wound our way up the mountain, we crossed an 11,500 foot pass and headed into Park County. Dawn was not going to be pretty. The sky was overcast and the wind was blowing hard. It was cold and I was glad to have on several layers of clothing, rented from the National Outdoor Leadership School outfitting shop in Lander, through the capable help of Kevin McGowan. NOLS has pioneered lightweight clothing that comes in layers and really keeps you warm in the high country.

We were riding up a narrow path along the spine of a mountain ridge. Below us, the land dropped hundreds of feet on each side.

Sheep hunting has been called by some "the hunt of the lucky." Sometimes, a bighorn ram will be waiting 100 yards from camp on opening day. But when that doesn't happen, you have to really work for it.

In truth, you spend hours and hours scanning the mountains through your binoculars and spotting scope. Your eyes get bleary and your neck gets stiff. You look and look. Then you look some more. You look in the morning and you look at night. You look everywhere, always hoping...

A FEW YEARS AGO, I competed in the World Musky Hunt in Lake Minocqua, Wisc. The musky is known as "the fish of 1,000 casts."

Well, my guide told me that a ram is known as "the animal who hides in 1,000 places." I certainly believed that after our hunting efforts that first week.

Now it is important to point out here that I am not one of those hunters who has waited all his life to hunt a bighorn sheep. I only applied as an afterthought this year (1993). When your brother-in-law is a sheep guide and encourages you to do it, well, you do it. But it sure was a big surprise to draw my permit.

It made me feel a little like a person who had just gotten his driver's license and his first road trip was the Indy 500.

My big game hunting experience had been limited to weekend hunting because the fall is the busiest time of year in the newspaper business. Unfortunately, I could never justify taking a week off to go hunting. This was going to be, essentially, a new experience.

I was very serious about getting a sheep, and I'd worked hard getting ready for the hunt. I drew some consolation when a lot of my friends told me about their unsuccessful sheep hunts.

I HAD BEEN WORKING OUT a lot at the local Wind River Fitness Center trying to get physically ready for the hunt. I knew it would be an endurance test, but frankly I wasn't prepared for how hard it would be. It seemed like I was always out of breath, huffing and puffing, up the sides of those mountains at that altitude.

One friend, Gary Barney, told me that hunting bighorn sheep was "a spiritual experience." He told me it would change me forever.

He may have been right. The scenery, thin air, worries about bears and scaling mountain summits did Christian-ize me, somewhat.

I did get to see some country unlike anything I had ever seen before. There was a virtual forest of petrified wood in one location at 11,000 feet. Strange, eerie rock formations jutted out of the sides of the mountains above timberline in other places we visited. We saw huge bull elk and lots of bighorn ewes and lambs. But no rams.

Standing on top of a 12,000 foot mountain in the Absarokas was a lot like standing on the rim of the Grand Canyon. When you looked at the mountains all around, they looked like vast canyons.

Unlike the Wind Rivers, the Absarokas seem crumbly. They feature long, narrow ridges that you can walk or ride a horse up. We scaled several summits on horseback, although my heart was often in my mouth as we did it. These were certainly the most sure-footed horses I had ever been around.

O UR PLAN HAD BEEN to get in a few days of early hunting at the opening of the season, which we did. If we weren't successful (we weren't), we'd go back later and get that ram.

Looking back and ahead, I can only say that a little luck would be nice. The alternative is a combination of hard work and spectacular experiences that aren't for the faint of heart.

(Note: I didn't get my sheep.)

Sage Grouse Struttin'

One of the West's oddest displays
by one of its more normal-acting birds
was going to happen
and we would witness it.

T HE BUZZER ON MY ALARM CLOCK pierced the darkness at 4 a.m. I groggily reached over and slammed down the button. It was just too early to get out of bed. I rolled over and went back to sleep.

Bzzzzzz went the persistent alarm. My wife Nancy poked me and said, "Either turn it off or get up, but keep that snooze alarm from going off!"

My plan was to join an expedition to view some sage grouse doing their annual strutting. And you need to get up early if you are going to see them. I am embarrassed to say that up to the present time, I had never seen this display. But this morning would be different. One of the West's oddest displays by one of its more normal-acting birds was going to happen and we would witness it.

The trip was probably provoked by the presence of our British newspaper intern Ben Russell. He and I were going to be hosted by that experienced birder Charlie Nations for this trip.

I really wanted to go back to sleep. As a reporter, I had had a late night meeting to cover the evening before, and I was operating on way too little sleep.

Finally, I dragged myself out of bed. Shortly, I was at the office to start our trip. Charlie brought along a thermos of coffee which helped shake the sleepiness out of my eyes.

We went to a place near Twin Creek on U. S. Highway 287 between Lander and Jeffrey City. Out in a field, we could see many little white bodies as the dawn started to turn the eastern sky a pale orange.

There must have been more than a hundred of the birds. They were strutting and making odd noises that Ben thought sounded like water droplets falling into an empty bucket.

The birds would blow themselves up to twice normal size and then strut around. Some even did a dance.

Still, to other birds it was high noon. They were literally dueling gunmen. They would take after each other and flap their wings against each other until one of them would retire, appearing somewhat droopy compared to his puffed-up victor.

OTHER PEOPLE who had viewed this group of grouse have had their sight-seeing experience interrupted by a golden eagle that would swoop down and scoop up one of the fat little birds for breakfast.

Needless to say, that usually put a damper on the birds' celebration. But there was no eagle this morning. The grouse danced, pranced and thunked for over an hour before we had enough photos and finally gave up and went back to town for some breakfast.

It was an interesting and informative trip and one that I would recommend to anyone here in Wyoming. Sleep is important, but you can always catch up on it later. The chance to see these birds perform comes along only rarely.

Spring in Yellowstone

Like much of Wyoming,
spring breaking here is a constant
tug-of-war, as Old Man Winter tries to
maintain his strong grip on the weather.

SPRING IN YELLOWSTONE PARK means many things. It means calves nuzzling bison cows. It means green grass in the geyser basins. Often it means snowdrifts. And most important, to us on this vacation, it means many animals and few people.

Yellowstone is just about my favorite place on the planet. But I had never visited it in spring.

On this Saturday, it looked a lot more like winter than it did spring. Then, Sunday dawned into a beautiful sunny day.

Like much of Wyoming, spring breaking here is a constant tug-of-war as Old Man Winter tries to maintain his strong grip on the weather. In Wyoming, winter doesn't just go away, it fights hard before bitterly relinquishing its grip. And perhaps nowhere in this state does it linger longer or more frequently than in our nation's oldest national park.

THE OLD FAITHFUL INN had only been open a couple of days. The workers were busy scrambling around, trying to do things right. It was like opening night at a theatre. The players were in their places, but the timing was occasionally off.

There is no other place in America quite like the Old Faithful Inn. Its nine-story open lobby is unique, especially when it is observed that it was built in 1904 and is made entirely of wood.

Architect Robert Reamer was just 29 years old when he designed it. Ahead of his time, he felt it should be built of the materials from the area where it existed and be natural. The open lobby style has been emulated in huge modern hotels all across America in the past few decades. In so many ways, this Inn was way ahead of its time.

The meals were wonderful in the dining room of this 90-year-old masterpiece. The service and quality were top-rate, especially when we recalled this was just their second day open.

Many of the rooms are the kind with the bathrooms and showers just down the hall. Many rooms also have bathrooms with tubs, but we found the hall system to be no inconvenience at all. It gave the place a sort of communal feeling to see people running around the halls in their bathrobes and jogging suits carrying their little shaving kits and make-up cases.

THE LATE JOHN TOWNSLEY always told me the best way to see Yellowstone is in the evening and early in the morning, both times from 6 to 9.

A former long-time Yellowstone Park Superintendent, he knew this was the time when the tourists weren't out — and the animals were.

Our little group followed his sage advice and our Sunday morning tour was true to his prediction. Elk, bison, moose, geese, swans and the sounds of many other animals were all over the place. We toured many of the geyser basins, including the largest in the world, Norris Basin. In the chill morning air, the geysers and hot springs were even more awesome as the steam dominated the vista. Often, our car was the only vehicle in the parking lots.

MY TRAVELOGUE can go on and on. As stated earlier, Yellowstone is one of my favorite places on the planet, and it is only three hours from Lander.

The Lake Hotel wasn't open yet and Yellowstone Lake was frozen over on this morning. The front lobby of that huge building is one of the most pleasant places in all of Wyoming, with its wicker furniture, windows overlooking the lake and piano music playing in the background.

On our way home, we spotted a grizzly bear about 100 feet off the main highway, just a few miles from the Lake Hotel. It was a chilling experience to see one of these beasts so close to where people like to be. Traffic, what little there was at this time of year, was backed up for some distance, as people stood in awe of this modern-day monster.

Once, we had to stop on the road as a huge bison slowly walked down the middle of our lane. He never stopped as he ponderously ambled on down the pavement.

Snowdrifts were very high near Yellowstone Canyon and our trip to Old Faithful was 60 miles longer than expected, because of highway construction on Craig Pass. It did give us a chance to see more of the park.

It snowed heavily on Togwotee Pass. It was hard to believe this was occurring on May 7.

Spring in Yellowstone is a beautiful time. It would be advisable for visitors, though, to pack their heavy coats and snow boots.

The worst job in the world?

Despite the stinking bear bait, this job reminded me a little of those scenes from skin divers who photograph sharks from inside heavy cages.

A PARK RANGER in Yellowstone Park took on a task one day a few years ago that ranked down among the worst jobs I've ever heard about. It involved danger, no escape hatch and smelly working conditions.

This is a follow-up to recent news items about grizzly bears that have been gaining in population in northwest Wyoming.

Besides attracting tourists, a female grizzly had attracted a male, and both needed to be to moved to safer parts of the park. The sow was called Number 134 and was well-known among National Park employees. She had been hanging around the Lake Hotel area for some time, which is where I photographed her during a weekend in May.

But lest local tourists get nervous, the Park Service in this instance removed old No. 134 to a different locale. The story about how they

162

did it and what they went through is quite interesting.

According to an article by Angus Thuermer of the *Jackson Hole News,* the female bear loved to fish. She has been known to scoop some 30 fish an hour out of the river. And she instinctively knew that there are eight streams between her home near Heart Lake and the Lake Hotel where spawning fish can be found.

Chief Ranger Dan Sholly was quoted as saying No. 134 had lost her fear of humans. But she really wasn't the biggest problem. The biggest problem was a huge male grizzly that was competing for her attentions.

This male, which apparently doesn't have a name or a number, followed No. 134 to the Lake Hotel area and started charging vehicles in jealousy. This bear, which rangers estimated to be over 400 pounds, made the situation "radically more dangerous," according to the report. Sholly said the bear was so big, a man might not be able to circle his neck with both arms.

With employees arriving and tourists converging on the Park, the behavior of this male was not good. "He was becoming very possessive of her," Sholly said. "That gave us great concern. Our concern became him."

THE PARK then activated its Bear Management Committee. Traps were set up for both bears without success. No. 134 was known to be wary of traps so rangers decided on a somewhat different approach, which prompted my observation about this being a terrible job.

Ranger Steve Frye took on one of the worst predicaments I have ever heard about. He climbed inside the bear trap, which contained putrid meat bait. Frye was armed with a tranquilizer gun and there he sat, and waited, and waited, and I assume . . . stunk and stunk and stunk. In fact, he must have stunk to high heaven. Maybe he was issued a gas mask. I don't know. But this is a brave man.

Despite the stinking bear bait, this job reminded me a little of those scenes of skin divers who photograph sharks from inside heavy cages.

Finally, old No. 134 lumbered nearby and Frye, probably nearly driven mad himself by the stench, nailed her from 20 yards with a drug dart and the bear collapsed.

Some delays occurred in trying to get the helicopter that they normally use to move comatose bears. It was being used for a mountain rescue. Finally, the helicopter arrived and the bear was moved to Heart Lake.

It was assumed the threatening male would now disappear from the area since the object of his attention was no longer around. This was the third time No. 134 had been moved from the Lake Hotel area.

IN THE MEANTIME, rangers have started an "aversive conditioning" process to teach the female to fear humans, again. This will involve playing a California bird call in the presence of human or automobile sounds while pelting the bear with dum-dum bullets. The bear learns to associate the people noises or the bird call with the pain, and it should learn to retreat whenever it hears either, according to the rangers.

It sounds like that has taken care of old No. 134. However, I don't know what kind of aversive conditioning Ranger Frye has been put through to restore him to normalcy.

Yellowstone's secret spots

Our purpose during this trip was
to see some of the lesser known sights.
We wanted to visit places
we hadn't visited before.

YELLOWSTONE NATIONAL PARK is the greatest place on earth. It offers a combination of natural wonders with a variety of unusual man-made hotels that is unparalleled on the planet.

Our family makes an annual pilgrimage to Yellowstone each year. This year, it wasn't until Labor Day that we finally made it. And despite intermittent snow, we experienced our typical fantastic time.

The Lake Hotel was superb as usual. In my mind, it is the finest hotel in existence. Sitting amid the wicker furniture and ferns in the sunroom, looking out at the vast lake with music from a grand piano in the background, is heaven for me.

Our purpose during this trip was to see some of the lesser known sights. We wanted to visit places we hadn't visited before.

The snow closing Dunraven Pass and the Beartooth Highway postponed part of our exploration for another time.

I want to share some of our most recent experiences:

• Our first destination was the great natural arch. It involves a one-mile hike off the main road. It is near Bridge Bay Marina. The walk was exhilarating, and the great arch is a huge natural stone bridge. It was discovered in 1880 by the Hayden expedition. It originally was destined to have a road cross it, but that plan was luckily squelched.

• Another side trip took us to Firehole Canyon. I don't know why we had never made this side trip before, but it was one of the high points of our trip. The waterfall is huge, and the cascades tumble down the canyon for miles. It is located near the West entrance.

• We visited the Virginia Cascades during the middle of a blinding snowstorm. It was blizzard-like and you could hardly see the road, making the whole experience a little nerve-wracking this early in the season. When I finally stopped and got out to take a photo, a man in a pickup stopped behind me. He had a big smile on his face when he came up to me.

"It's a good thing we're locals," he laughed. "This would scare the devil out of some Southerner, wouldn't it?" He was from Twin Bridges, Montana, and we agreed that Labor Day was for locals. Indeed, the park was full, but mainly with cars from Wyoming, Montana and Idaho.

The Cascades were gorgeous. It was the first time we had seen them since our first Yellowstone trip 22 years ago. And this was my first time in winter!

• I love Yellowstone's Grand Canyon. It seems like we never have enough time to stand there and appreciate the views. This time, we took a different route and visited a place called Uncle Tom's Trail. We saw the third waterfall in the canyon for the first time. It was spectacular and almost embarrassing that I had not viewed the canyon waterfalls from there before.

• We visited Firehole Lake for the first time. It is a huge boiling stretch of water just north of Old Faithful on the east side of the road. With major geyser basins on the west side, like Biscuit, Lower and Middle basins, it has always been easy to overlook this small lake. It was very impressive and worth the visit.

ONE OF THE FIRST THINGS I DO after checking into the Lake Hotel is go down to the lake and just watch that vast body of water. On this Saturday evening, the lake was churning. Whitecaps were everywhere and there were just a few boats.

It didn't take long before Nancy gave up and said she and Michael were going in, it was too cold. That left just me and another guy sitting there on the benches looking out over this huge, inland sea. "It's beautiful here," he hollered over to me. I walked over and said I agreed with him. He laughed that my family had deserted me. His had, too. It was just too brisk. But he loved this view. It reminded him of the sea.

His name was Ray Marino and he had just returned home from a stretch of time on a carrier near Yugoslavia. His wife treated him to a trip to Wyoming that included a stay at the Jackson Lake Lodge and now the Lake Hotel. I complimented him on her good taste. It was his first trip to Wyoming and he was overwhelmed.

I was impressed by his story. He lives in Chicago and at 38, had been reactivated by the Marines for the Gulf War a year ago. He flew 196 missions into Iraq from carriers. He flew F-14s and was naturally proud of how well the planes flew. He said what sets Americans apart from other countries is our obsession with maintenance. "Everything worked just like it was supposed to," he said.

BUT HERE HE WAS IN WYOMING, enjoying Yellowstone Park for the first time.

With the wind blowing in his hair, he was standing by the railing looking off at the mountains and a rainbow in the distance. It was a long way from strife and the deck of an aircraft carrier.

Fires scorched Yellowstone

Most Wyoming mountains were blacked
out by haze from all the fires,
but the sunsets were really spectacular.
The smoke always created the most
unusual effect on the setting sun.

REMEMBER 1988'S MILD, DRY SPRING? Or that record hot June? We reaped a dubious harvest from those two events in July that year, as Wyoming forests burned up.

Yellowstone Park burned at a rate unseen in its recorded history. Fires popped up all around northwest Wyoming. Two fires even burned above Lander that summer.

One fire expert predicted we were in "for a helluva summer" and he was right. Luckily, the entire place didn't go up in blazes.

Occasionally when we have dry springs, our summers can be wet. But not in 1988. Storms over Yellowstone spawned way more lightning than rain that summer, which sparked many of the fires.

The South entrance to the park soon closed, which could certainly cause a negative economic impact on places like Fremont County that feed that gate.

And the whole country soon learned about the fires in Yellowstone. That story was being headlined in all the nation's major newspapers and was the lead story on the night-time TV newscasts. Most Wyoming mountains were blacked out by haze from all the fires, but the sunsets were really spectacular. The smoke always created the most unusual effect on the setting sun.

MY MOST EXCITING EVENT THAT SUMMER was a flight when I took my airplane over the Park during the height of the firestorm.

Smoke covered everything and fire would shoot hundreds of feet into the air.

One of the densest areas of smoke was the huge Yellowstone Lake where the cold air from the water would attract the smoke.

It was an overwhelming experience to be able to see nothing but smoke and fire in all directions as far as the eye could see.

People who read my writings know how much I love Yellowstone Park. And on that day, I was watching it burn up.

It was like watching a loved one die. And you knew there was nothing you could do about it, except mourn.

Yellowstone dazzles foreign journalists

Wyomingites are lucky to live in a marvelous state that includes a magical place like Yellowstone. It is my favorite place in the world, which qualifies me as a pretty good tour guide.

"BEEL, DO YOU REALIZE how lucky you are to live near such a place?"

That question was posed to me a few years ago while taking four European journalists on a tour of Yellowstone National Park. They were in Jackson Hole attending a conference and wanted to see the planet's oldest national park first-hand. Lucky for me, I was their tour guide.

Heinz Tomek, head of the Austrian News Service, and Adrian Weber, an author and reporter from Luxembourg, sat in the front seat of the rented mini-van.

Beside and behind me were two occasionally cantankerous Israeli reporters who aggressively disagreed with each other on almost everything. They were Uri Dan, a veteran reporter for the *New York Post* and Yossi Sarid, the most "dovish" member of the Israel Knesset (Parliament). Sarid is an author and founder of the most respected political magazine in his country.

Wyomingites are lucky to live in a marvelous state that includes a magical place like Yellowstone. It is my favorite place in the world, which qualifies me as a pretty good tour guide. I am always surprised by people's reactions to the wonders of the big park. This was going to be an interesting trip.

Yossi was speechless at the beauty of the Grand Canyon of Yellowstone. It was one of those classic Wyoming fall days when the sky is a deep blue with a bright yellow sun peeking through occasional wisps of white clouds. There was very little wind and the power of the Upper Falls enveloped us. Yossi turned to me and said, "This is the most beautiful place I have ever seen. It is all so clear. The air is so pure."

The power of the waterfall was dizzying as the water relentlessly flowed over the cliff in front of us and tumbled to the pool below.

ALL FOUR MEN were heavy smokers and heavy coffee drinkers although they complained about how weak American coffee can be.

It was amusing to see the lunch ordered by Uri and Yossi. Both ordered a chili meal and then poured Tabasco sauce over the chili. No ulcers for these folks, I surmised. They were debating each other constantly, usually in Hebrew. Yet when they weren't arguing, they were genuinely friendly.

Our next stop was the Norris Geyser Basin, which is the largest such thermal area in the world. It has a science fiction feel about it as you descend into this strange area of bubbling water, steam, shooting geysers and unstable ground.

"Beel," Uri said. "One half hour ago, you take us to heaven. Now you take us to hell! And we thought we lived in the land of the Bible." Other comments ranged from "Fellini must have designed this place," to "So, you have your Dead Sea, too."

Uri and Yossi are both addicts of CNN. They say they can't live without it and were stunned to find a place in America without television sets. The conference was at Jackson Lake Lodge where the cabins don't have TVs.

After three days, Uri said he was "finally getting weaned from CNN, but it is very, very difficult."

OUR TOUR CONTINUED. I told them about Colter's Hell and the Lewis and Clark Expedition and why the Park was created in the first place. And we talked about the history of the Lake Hotel and Old Faithful Inn and why bears were so scarce.

But the fires baffled them. They had all heard about the 1988 fires but stared in disbelief at the extent of the damage still covering the forests and mountainsides during this 1990 trip. The vast size of the blaze was beyond their comprehension and the stark areas of burned timber depressed them. "How could something so awful happen in a place so beautiful?" Heinz asked. They were all familiar with the answer that this was supposedly nature's way, but they just couldn't buy it.

I was surprised at their reaction to the fires. I have always felt Yellowstone's great wonders really did not involve the forest anyway. To me the fires were tragic, but the parts of Yellowstone that I love the most were still intact.

While leaving the park, we spotted a huge bull elk with three cows. My tour group, over my objections, was able to get fairly close in the dense timber and watch in awe. The monarch easily moved through the closely-aligned trees without hitting them with his antlers.

Then the bull elk started to bugle. It raised the hair on the back of my neck. What a wonderful, wilderness-type of sound. My friends were paralyzed in their tracks. "Why is he making that strange noise?" they asked.

I wanted to answer "Because he was so happy to live in such a place," and maybe, in a way, that was true. It would have sounded better than to just say he was wooing cows.

Where the wind never blows

⟹━◈━⟸

"There's no wind here," she remarked, which prompted my favorite story about Lander being one of the 10 unwindiest cities in the United States.

⟹━◈━⟸

TUESDAY, A BUREAU CHIEF for the *Philadelphia Inquirer* visited Lander while writing a story on the energy bust in Wyoming.

To help out the Chamber of Commerce, I showed her around our valley. This reporter, Fawn Vrazo, had spent some time in Casper and Jeffrey City before arriving here.

She said she could not get those images of Jeffrey City out of her mind. "It's just incredible to see a modern day ghost town like that," she said. She said people there told her the town had gone from 5,000 people to about 70.

Although she is based in Houston, which has certainly had a bust of its own, she had not seen such economic devastation in her travels.

But the good news was that she couldn't get over the beauty and scenery of Lander Valley. While here, we toured some of the economic bright spots in Lander, such as Eagle Bronze.

Nary a leaf was moving as we drove around. "There's no wind here," she remarked, which prompted my favorite story about Lander being one of the 10 unwindiest cities in the United States. "Boy, Casper and Jeffrey City were sure windy," she remarked.

It was so nice, she promised to come back in the summer with her husband and young son. Perhaps they would spend a few more days in Lander on their way to Yellowstone Park.

She headed for Evanston from here, and I only hope that she didn't come back through Lander during the latter part of the week.

Otherwise, she probably would have asked me some pertinent questions about our weather, like, "What is that sound you hear? What is that energy force that almost knocked you down? What was that thing that just went flying by? It looked like a person?"

Why, it couldn't have been our 60 mph wind?

Remember, the wind doesn't blow in Lander!

Snowmobiling in Lander is spectacular

Once on top, the trail was groomed
smooth. With good visibility
and no wind,
it was possible to really cruise.

THE AIR WAS CRISP. The sky was blue. The snow was plentiful. It was a great day for snowmobiling in the Wind River Mountains in west-central Wyoming near Lander.

That Sunday afternoon four years ago offered a good opportunity to get out my creaky old snowmobile, bundle up and head for the trails. My young son Michael rode behind as we took off up the switchbacks toward Louis Lake on the Loop Road.

The parking lot was nearly full at Bruce's Camp in Sinks Canyon. Obviously, we weren't the only ones thinking snowmobiling.

The ride up the mountain on the switchbacks was exceptionally bumpy. These bumps are called moguls and if you took them too fast, they could would shake fillings out of your teeth. But who could complain? It was a great day.

Once on top, the trail was groomed smooth. With good visibility and no wind, it was possible to really cruise. We didn't go nearly as

175

fast as many of the other riders on their snowmobiles, but it would be possible to go at a high rate of speed for a long ways on some of the vast meadows. The Loop Road, with snow packed on it, is much smoother than it is in the summer. With the development of the snowmobile, it doesn't take as long to get where you want to go in the winter as in the summer.

Our compliments to the grooming crew. It would be impossible to keep the moguls down on the switchbacks coming up out of Sinks Canyon, as too many snowmobilers are gunning their machines off and on to get up the hill. But once on top, the road was smooth as ice. The money for grooming comes from the permits people buy each year for their snowmobiles.

A special treat was a little side trip off the road near Blue Ridge. That area is some 9,600 feet above sea level and is the highest point on the Loop Road. Just 200 yards east from the road down a familiar trail is a lookout that gives the viewer an awesome sight. We could see all the way across the Wind River Basin. It was a spectacular surprise. There was no indication that such a viewing area is so close to the Loop Road at that spot, which is almost two miles high in elevation.

The Maxon Basin Trail along the Loop Road also provides scenic views of huge Lizard Head Mountain, which is one of the most dramatic rock edifices in Wyoming. Lizard Head dominates a famous area called the "Cirque of the Towers."

THE LOOP ROAD TRAIL is the gateway to the famous Continental Divide Snowmobile Trail. As that trail gains in popularity, we will see many more winter-time tourists.

As this book goes to press, signs are more encouraging that soon the trail will go all the way from Lander to Yellowstone National Park, making it the most scenic trail in the world, in my opinion.

Ready for January thawing

"My feet are cold."
"Well, all you have to do is go to bed
and have a brick at your feet."
"I tried that."
"Did you get the brick hot?"
"Get it hot? It took all night
just to get it warm."

WYOMING PEOPLE HAD SHIVERED and trudged through a long wintry period a few years ago and were anxiously awaiting the annual January thaw.

The mercury has been below zero most mornings in my neighborhood and the only time it warmed up was so that it could snow again. We had more than 50 inches of snow so far that winter with more forecast. I am not really complaining. I like winter. Wyoming has the most beautiful winters in the world. A typical snowfall is so light and fluffy, it offers a spectacular beauty.

It's just that a little, bitty break in the weather would be okay to a great many people who live in Wyoming.

WYOMING PEOPLE had enjoyed sensationally mild winter weather for the past few years at the time that I wrote this. Except for occasional snowfalls and rare sub-zero spells, the winters were pretty open and darned mild.

Lander Valley appeared to be more a winter golfing haven at times rather than a snowmobiling capital.

But this particular year, it became its destiny as a snowmobiling capital. People headed to the mountains in record numbers.

In an effort to capitalize on the snowmobiling reputation, Lander city fathers passed an ordinance that allowed driving snowmobiles in the streets. However, the snowmobiling on the streets didn't really materialize. There were few snowmobiles seen on our streets.

MEANWHILE, THE SNOWFALL AND TEMPERATURES have contributed to record numbers of ice fishermen and snowmobilers.

This valley is famous for being a winter wonderland. We are not complaining, that's for sure.

But a little thawing in January would be nice for many folks.

Mountain Showers

⟫◦⟪

People protect what they love.
— *Jacques Cousteau*

⟫◦⟪

I HEARD MY SON hollering at me through the trees.

"Where are you?" he was asking.

"I'm up here," I replied, calling down to him from my perch on a big rock.

The scene was between rain showers on a hill overlooking Fiddler's Lake one Sunday afternoon in May a few years ago. The view was spectacular, looking down on this lake, which lies along the Loop Road in the Wind River Mountains above Lander. The water was so still, the trees on the other side were perfectly reflected in the glass-like lake surface.

"Oh, there you are. I see you found a 'thinking rock,'" he said, with a big smile on his face.

You see, "thinking rocks" aren't just ordinary rocks. These are those wonderful big, comfortable rocks that you can occasionally find on a mountainside or on a river bank. I would love to have one in my backyard, but I don't.

"So, dad, what are thinking about, way up here?" he asked.

"Well, son, I am pondering how you and I own all the land out there in front of us," I told him. "This is our spread." As far as our eyes could see was the Shoshone National Forest. The huge two-million-acre forest belongs to me and Michael and about 280,000,000 other people, too.

It's a great spread. It also is the oldest National Forest on the planet. It is a special place.

HE SAT DOWN BESIDE ME on his own rock and we looked around together. Then we got up and started exploring. We found small trees growing out of the centers of two separate rocks. We speculated just how old those little trees were to have survived growing out of a tiny crack in a rock.

From our vantage point, we could see for miles. Off to our right, we could see the smoke from many campfires. The sound of families enjoying the holiday filtered through the forest. The late afternoon sun sparkled through the wet leaves of the trees like so many diamonds.

Off to our left, one solitary family was making a lot of racket with a dirt bike. I should never complain about such noise, since I like to ride both snowmobiles and all-terrain vehicles, but on this particular afternoon, the noise was a little distracting. Soon it quit, though, and the only noise was a quickening wind rustling down the hillside.

The sky clouded over again and we decided to head back down to camp. We, along with wife Nancy, had planned to make it an overnighter but a few more looks at the oncoming rainstorm turned my spine yellow. We hadn't really set up camp yet, anyway, and it was almost as easy to load up and head out than to try to imagine what kind of night we would spend at that spot next to the lake.

The prospect of snow didn't seem entirely out of the question at that time of year in that place. The sky continued to get black as we loaded up.

With memories of my thinking rock diminishing and my mountain growing smaller in my rear mirror, we tucked our tails between our legs and headed home.

That night, while sleeping snugly in my bed, I listened to the heavy rain pounding the roof of our home. My guilt about giving up on our first night of mountain camping this particular season disappeared along with my wakened state.

Land
of
10,000 trails

As we were walking along, it occurred
to me that there could be 10,000 trails
like this one in the Lander vicinity in
these mountains. What a joy it was to
be out in the mountains on this day,
even for this brief time.

WITH RELATIVES IN TOW and my camera in hand, I sneaked out of
my office one Thursday afternoon and headed for the mountains.
"I'm going to shoot some photos," I told the rest of the *Journal* staff,
and left with a guilty conscience as they were all left there working.

By 4:30, we were starting up the Loop Road switchbacks in Sinks
Canyon outside of Lander, and by 5 p.m., we were hiking down an
unnamed trail west of Frye Lake. We were on a jeep trail that followed
a beautiful stream.

It was a brief trip and soon it was time to return home. But I had
given my relatives a brief look at our Wind River Mountains and it
had pleased them immensely.

As we were walking along, it occurred to me that there could be 10,000 trails like this one in the Lander vicinity in our part of Wyoming. What a joy it was to be out in the clear air on this day, even for this brief time.

I believe a big part of tourism future could be in walking trails.

NOW I AM NOT ADVOCATING that we immediately build 10,000 walking trails here in Wyoming but people need to be aware of the difference between hiking trails and walking trails. There is tremendous potential for both, but I would predict that walking trails could be the biggest tourist attraction of all.

We must, though, keep in mind environmental considerations when inviting people to hike in our mountain or desert areas, which can be very fragile.

The people of this country have joined their European cousins in adopting the walking craze. It is often called "trekking" over there.

WALKING TRAILS have been created all over the world. In Great Britain, there are extensive walking clubs with organized trail systems and programs where walkers earn points by the numbers of trails they walk.

All over Europe, tourists flock to their favorite trails on weekdays and weekends for their exercise. The trails usually aren't that long, perhaps two to ten miles.

In my travels around the world, it is not unusual at all to see people riding on airplanes with their trusty walking sticks in their hands.

People involved in developing our tourism potential here need to be aware of the future when it comes to walking trails. The potential is immense and would have a positive effect on our state's economy here.

THOUSANDS OF WYOMING PEOPLE are walking every day, too.

Here in Fremont County where I live, if you look around in Lander, Riverton, Dubois, Fort Washakie, Ethete, Shoshoni or South Pass, you can see people walking at all hours of the day. "Volksmarching" is another example of how walking is catching on in the state. Volksmarches are being held all over Wyoming at various times of year.

Walking is the exercise of the 1990s. Doctors have cautioned people for many years to watch out for the hazards of running or jogging. Most people tend to be overweight and tend to be out of shape. Many persons over 35 can hurt themselves by running. But not by walking, caution many doctors.

Walking is good for you. Doctors have been telling people to get off that couch and go for a walk. It ranks second only maybe to swimming as the least physically destructive way to improve heart and lung capacity.

And people all over America are listening to this advice.

So WITH THAT SAID, here are the opportunities by increasing our overall awareness of walking:

• Walking is good for people. It makes them healthier and happier.

• It is a good tourism draw. People would come here by the thousands for the opportunities to walk in our hills, mountains, deserts, valleys, canyons and meadows.

• Walking gets people away from their couches in front of the TV and gets them out talking to their neighbors and friends.

As A WYOMING COMMUNITY, we need to keep in mind the wonderful benefits of increasing our state trails system for walking and hiking. We could be a national leader in developing an organized trails system. And it probably wouldn't cost much, either.

So, get off that couch and take a walk!

Fishing

The worst day fishing is better than the best day working.

BULL LAKE is a magnificent body of water.

It stretches out nine miles along a huge gash cut into the mountains on the northern end of the Wind River Indian Reservation. And the fishing there is legendary.

Dan Kinneman of Dubois took my son Michael and me for a real fishing trip there one summer day in 1992. We were able to catch four huge lake trout (about 18" in length) plus catch and release a few rainbow trout.

It took most of the day to catch these big fish. Kinneman is an outfitter and fishing guide when he is not catering to his relatives. (He is my brother-in-law.) I can vouch for his abilities. It was a hot and difficult day and we cruised all over that 100-foot deep lake looking for fish. But he found them and we caught them.

The weather was so hot, Michael and Dan's dog, Darcy, spent part of the day swimming around next to the beaches.

THE TRIP DESCRIBED ABOVE is one of our more elaborate fishing trips taken here in Wyoming.

The most fun has been spending those lazy summer days along a rushing stream or a high mountain lake just keeping your line wet and reeling in an occasional fish.

It's at those times that a person can appreciate the tranquility that exists in Wyoming's high country. The settings are so natural. Often you are standing in a location that could have jumped off the front of a calendar on a Kansas barber shop wall. People who don't get to live in Wyoming or have never visited these high mountain vistas find it hard to believe that such places exist. But they do, here in The Best Part Of America.

I COULDN'T WRITE any fishing article without including the following true story:

As a small boy, growing up in a small town in Iowa, I would often sit along the bank of the river and fish. While sitting there, I would look up at the airplanes flying overhead and say to myself, I wish I could be there right now.

Today, since I travel so much in my various projects, I am often in the plane flying over the countryside. Often I look down, and if I see some young boy there, sitting along the river bank — fishing — I wish I could be there right now.

The great hunt

It costs $2,700 to make a phone call to heaven from New York. In Wyoming, it costs 73 cents. Why the difference? In Wyoming, it's a local call.

MY BROTHER RON and I spent a whole Sunday a few years ago deer hunting above Lander in the Wind River Mountains. As frequent readers of my columns already know, this will be one of those "isn't it great to be alive here in Wind River Country" columns. And it is.

We started hunting in 20-degree, crisp air along the face of the mountains and encountered ankle-deep snow higher up. When the sun came out, it was brilliant. You had to shade your eyes when you looked to the east, it was so bright.

It was chilly up at Suicide Point south of Lander. I was already breathing hard from the altitude and being out of shape, but the view back to the Wind River Basin really took my breath away.

I made the cardinal sin of accidentally leaving my camera home. Packing all the gear necessary for hunting (and for lunch!) must have contributed to that omission. So I will attempt to describe the scene.

The high point of the trip occurred at a slightly lower point, elevation-wise, in a big grove of pine and aspen trees near Baldwin Creek Canyon.

Our view looked off between two notches of another canyon near Mexican Creek. Spread out in front of us was the vast Wind River Basin, which was in a shadow except for Crowheart Butte, which jutted up in golden splendor.

Behind it towered white mountains, dominated by the snow-covered Washakie Needles. The sky was so clear, we were looking at least 75 to 100 miles.

After passing through the forest, we reached a clearing above the face of the Wind Rivers and walked over to peer down into Baldwin Creek Canyon. Evidence of deer and elk was everywhere. And the sounds of rifle shots indicated others were having better luck than we were.

This was my first view of Lander from that spot. After looking up at that canyon from Lander Valley for 20 years, it was fun to finally be able to look back down from up there.

Our outing was successful, by the way, and we'll be going out again next year.

We also harvested some deer.

Seven

The Future

The trouble with our times
is that the future
is not what it used to be.
—*Paul Valéry*

Boom time in the Rockies

The Rockies, perhaps too rosily, are increasingly being regarded as the new American heartland. They hold out a promise — not just of scenery and jobs — but also, most importantly, of old, back-country values and certainties.

THE COVER STORY of *Time Magazine* said it only too well:

"It's boom time in the Rockies. While most of the U. S. is suffering from the blues, or stuck in an outright funk like California, the six states along the spectacular spine of the Rockies — from Montana in the north through Idaho, Wyoming, Colorado and Utah to New Mexico in the south — are prospering happily. This is the good news belt."

The article in the nation's largest weekly news magazine spends eight pages plus the cover telling the world why it is so great to move to our part of the West.

The writers describe the new kind of commuters — telecommuters — who do their business by computer, telephone, fax and modem. We know people like that who live here in Fremont County already. They are already here. And more of them are coming.

The article continues:

"The Rockies, perhaps too rosily, are increasingly being regarded as the new American heartland. They hold out a promise — not just of scenery and jobs — but also, most importantly, of old, back-country values and certainties — like home, hearth and family — that have seemingly gone astray in many urban centers."

ONE OF THE HIDDEN TRENDS in business these days has been a wage-paying program called "payment for production" instead of paying for attendance. If a person produces, he or she gets paid in accordance with what is produced. Companies have found that once this principle is in place, workers don't need to be located in some centralized facility in some urban center. Thus, workers on projects can be located on a mountainside in Wyoming, for example.

As *Time* predicts, this trend toward telecommuting workers is just getting started. The small trickle will become a torrent. And places like Fremont County and Wyoming will see a great many new faces here as a result.

TOP TOWN!
Lander fifth best
small city in USA

So take an armchair trip to where the
American dream is alive and
well…where initiative and hard work
are still the keys to success, where good
manners and neighborly hospitality are
still prized, and where people will have
the roll-up-your-sleeves spirit that made
this country great.

— Norman Crampton, from the book
The 100 Best Small Towns in America

What a great recognition for Lander and Wyoming!

A nationally-recognized study has verified what we already
know: Lander is one of the top five towns in America. We think it
is the best, but we'll settle for being in the top 100 and listed as fifth
best.

The book quoted above hit the news in February, 1993, with the author appearing on national TV and stories about his findings appearing in all major newspapers. While being interviewed by *Good Morning America* on ABC-TV, Crampton had this to say about Lander:

> *Lander, Wyoming, is a fabulous small town near the Rockies. In fact, it is in the Rockies. They recovered from a disastrous loss of jobs. They're doing great. They have a great climate. It's a real nice town.*

WE ALL KNOW about Lander's great natural attributes. The mountains, the proximity to national parks, national forest, great deserts, the Oregon Trail, the Indian reservation and our other natural benefits.

Then there is our weather—our lack of wind, low humidity and 300 sunny days per year—something that has no parallel in the Rocky Mountains.

The endorsements given to Lander by four of our citizens are included in the book. All four, Linda Hewitt, Tom Bell, Cathy Purves and Chavawn Woodall Kelly, offered readers of this book an insightful look at our town. The *Journal* and this editor were listed repeatedly in the book, and, as a result, the newspaper has received dozens of calls and letters. More than 800 people have contacted the Chamber of Commerce about moving to Lander.

BUT THAT ISN'T WHAT PUT LANDER over the top in comparison with literally thousands of other towns in America.

It is a combination of how Lander rebounded from economic peril and how it fares in comparative indicators with other small cities and towns.

Lander bounced back from a devastating economic crash in the 1980s when more than a thousand jobs disappeared and more than 50 percent of the local economy vanished with iron and uranium mining jobs.

From a depressing total of more than 500 homes for sale, Lander now has fewer than 30. Virtually all economic indicators tell stories about this community's robust health.

ON A SERIES OF COMPARISONS, here is how Lander scored when compared with the other 99 towns (the lower the score, the better):

Growth rate (1980-90)	100th
Per capita income	40th
Residents ages 25-34	5th
Percentage non-white pop.	20th
Crime rate	73rd
Doctors in county	17th
College educated people	24th
Education expenditures	4th
SUMMARY	5TH

Note: the percentage of non-white population was considered to be an advantage as it promoted cultural diversity, which we agree with.

WE COULD ARGUE with two of the columns. His growth rate is wrong because Crampton used the wrong population figures for 1980, and Lander fares much higher in the doctor to population ratio if it were counted just as the town and not as the county. In both areas, we deserve a much better rating. Lander probably would have emerged as number one had those figures been accurate.

But who is complaining! It is a time to celebrate this wonderful recognition.

Message to graduates

The best news for this generation, compared to their parents' generation, is that they are living in a time when great peace has spread all over the earth. What a wonderful time this could be.

E VERY YEAR IN MAY, I try to write an editorial aimed at all those high school seniors who are graduating and heading out into the real world. It is one of my favorite annual messages.

It is dedicated to all these young people who are wondering "what is going to happen to me?"

We honor these young people who have finished the first leg of their educational careers.

While many graduates are confused about their careers, I applaud all the young people who seem to have their lives lined out at this point. They are to be admired. But they need to be aware that some statistical studies indicate that the average senior graduating will have four different careers in the course of his or her lifetime. That statistic can be either very interesting or very sobering.

In the information-driven, computer-generated, service-oriented global economy we live in today, who can accurately predict what the future holds for any of us?

WE LIVE IN A TIME when even middle-aged people are changing careers. This is a time when millions of Americans have been forced to change jobs when their careers should be blossoming. These changes are due to foreign competition, mega-mergers, corporate cutbacks and government program cuts.

Poet Carl Sandburg had numerous careers with the most impressive being that of biographer and poet. He described his life 50 years ago:

> *I am an idealist. I don't know*
> *where I am going, but I'm on my way.*

TODAY'S HIGH SCHOOL SENIORS are on their way, too. They venture forth into a world much different from that of their parents.

Most of the seniors I know are more conservative than their parents were, when it comes to careers and jobs. These seniors have seen the economic chaos that has occurred in this country in the past decade. Because of what they have seen, I believe the members of this generation will be very cautious and very successful. They will work hard and they will work smart.

The smart worker will be the one who keeps track of national and international trends. There will be tremendous opportunities in industries such as tourism and travel. International commerce will continue to grow, offering lucrative and exciting jobs.

Those people who master foreign languages and learn about international trade and financial skills could be guaranteed good careers. Agriculture will also offer tremendous world-wide opportunities, we would predict.

And there will continue to be tremendous opportunities in the service economy. In a country where both parents often work, there will be many entrepreneurial opportunities for those people who specialize in providing a service, whether it be greasing a car, cleaning a home, babysitting children or offering specialized tutoring skills.

THE BEST NEWS FOR THIS GENERATION, compared to their parents' generation, is that they are living in a time when great peace has spread all over the earth. What a wonderful time this could be, compared to the Cold War anxieties endured by us, your parents.

You don't have a Vietnam War to worry about. Or a Cuban missile crisis. Or an Iron Curtain that inhibits world-wide attempts to feed the hungry and aid the poor.

Today, this generation has it in its power to live during a time when peace and democracy reign all over the globe. My advice is to pay attention to world events and to help out wherever you can. And I would conclude with this quote from one of our generation's more optimistic people, who said:

Every child is nature's chance to correct culture's error.

New roles
for men

Ed Porthan sees the time coming
when men will not be afraid
to show their feelings.

"SOME MINDS ARE LIKE CONCRETE — all mixed up and permanent-
ly set," Ed Porthan joked during a seminar at the end of Men's Health
Week, held a few years ago at the Lander Valley Medical Center.

Porthan, who is executive director of the Minnesota Administrators Academy in St. Paul, Minn., presented a two-hour program
called "Maximizing your Masculinity" to about 30 men.

He said he was pleased to be back in Lander. Porthan served as
curriculum director of the local high school for eight years.

"PARADIGM SHIFTS ARE OCCURRING," he told the group. He referred
to changes in the way people think. Specifically, he talked about how
men are thinking about themselves and about how they are supposed
to act.

He had members of the group summarize their thoughts about
people who served as their mentors in their early life. He wrote
words like "friendly, loving, trusting and fair" on the board as people
shouted them out. Then he had the men come up with words to
describe their relationships with their fathers in their early years,
using three good words and three bad words. Words like "temperamental, rigid and macho" were put on the board.

Porthan pointed out that as the generations age, a shift in thinking is also occurring. He sees the time coming when men will not be afraid to show their feelings. He also said men will enjoy showing their feelings, such as hugging their children, which he used as an example.

He quoted a well-known business consultant who described the business of the future would operate with four big f-words and two small f-words, he said.

The big ones would be, first, "Focused. If you don't know where you are going, any road can take you there," he said.

Second, is "Fast. You have got to move fast in today's world. Committees are like dodo birds," he claimed.

Third, is "Flexible. You can't be rigid," he said. "Even our perceptions can be fixed."

Fourth is "Friendly. Antagonism just won't make it in today's world," he said.

The two small f's are "family and fun," he said.

SOME OTHER PEARLS OF WISDOM used by Porthan were as follows:
- "Power doesn't diminish when you give it away, it generates more power. When somebody keeps it, power diminishes."
- "Anything worth doing is worth doing poorly the first time."
- "We move toward and become what we think about most."
- "Marshall McLuhan said, 'Most people ride through life looking through their rear view mirror.'"
- "Competition depresses creativity. Cooperation increases it."
- "'A breakthrough is usually preceded by a breakdown,' said Jean Houston."
- "The IQ test is a bogus instrument."
- "When the receiver gets ready, the messenger comes."
- "It is estimated that 80 percent of all cancer is caused by stress."
- "Sometimes people would rather stay with a familiar pain than try an unfamiliar pleasure."

Higher ground

›-0-‹

These are the times.
We are the people.
If not now, when?
If not you, who?
— *Jean Houston,*
an acclaimed behavior scientist

›-0-‹

IN THE PRESS OF DAY-TO-DAY LIFE, how does one find a few moments occasionally to take a bigger look at the world? When does one attempt to find a higher ground in the way we work, play or live?

Like a bug in a rug, life can be pretty secure here in Wyoming. We are tucked away in our mountains. It seems we are so far away from world problems such as oil spills, famine, AIDS and economic strife.

Or are we?

Are there things we can do to make the world a better place, even here in Lander? Can writing a letter for Amnesty International help out? Or collecting money for UNICEF? Or getting involved with the unemployed in our community. Or even picking up trash?

A reporter once said to Mother Teresa: "What difference are you making? You save a few starving children. It's just a drop in the ocean." She replied: "Yes, it's just a drop in the ocean. But if I didn't do it, there'd be one less drop."

Wyoming people live in a unique place where individual people can make a difference. We are lucky in that we are not surrounded by millions of people rushing around making us feel insignificant. For all citizens here in Wyoming should feel significant, if only because of our low population.

People can get involved in political races. Or philosophical choices. Or being a Big Brother or Big Sister. Or a volunteer to a hospital or a nursing home. Or a suicide hotline.

There are lots of other ways people can help out, either singly or in groups.

"Never doubt that a small group of thoughtful, committed citizens can change the world. Indeed, it's the only thing that ever has," said Margaret Mead. That is how a small group like Amnesty International became a Nobel Peace Prize-winning international group that has freed thousands of political prisoners worldwide.

Former President Dwight Eisenhower showed he could predict the future very accurately when he pointed out: "One day the people of the world will want peace so badly that the governments will have to get out of their way and let them have it." Perhaps that is happening now. Let us rejoice in it, but keeping working at it.

MEANWHILE, ON A LOCAL LEVEL, there are projects such as creating jobs, cleaning up the community and working with our Native American friends. All will involve time, but persons of good will can find the time to do good things.

Even coaching a Little League team or helping a Scout troop are ways of providing depth to your community. Anything to do with children would probably rank as our highest priority.

THE FOLLOWING STANZAS of a popular song sum up a way of life worth striving for:

There are those who can live
with the things they don't believe in.
They are giving up their lives for something that is less than it can be.

Some have longed for a home
in a place of inspiration.
Some will find emptiness inside
By giving it all for the things
that they believe.

Maybe it's just a dream in me
Maybe it's just my style.
Maybe it's just the freedom that I have found.

Given the possibility
of living up to the dream in me
You know that I'll be reaching for the higher ground.

— John Denver, from the song *Higher Ground*

A message to the future

Service to humanity
is our culture's highest calling.
When all our days are done,
the true measure of our lives will not be
what we had or what we owned,
but rather who we helped.

Note: Back in 1990, Wyoming's centennial year, a time capsule was placed in a waterproof cement box at Sinks Canyon State Park.

During the ceremonies on that day, I read the following statement and included a printed version that was placed inside the time capsule. It went something like the following:

HELLO THERE, ALL OF YOU, somewhere off in the future! We hope you're doing fine. We're doing pretty well, too, back here in 1990.

That is our opening message to the people who will read this editorial 100 years from now when they open the Sinks Canyon Time Capsule that is being buried here.

Wyoming will boom in the next 100 years, and I predict that Lander will be a recreational hub of a county that contains some 150,000 people. It will be five times as crowded in 100 years as it is today. And that figure may be conservative.

You people in the future who now live where we live today are no doubt enjoying it nearly as much as we did. You are probably doing things in ways that we can only imagine today.

A favorite saying is:

We didn't inherit the earth from our parents;
We are borrowing it from our children.

That always made a lot of sense. I hope the world you live in offers a sustainable lifestyle. If all the efforts made in the 20th century pay off, as we hope, you don't live in a poisoned environment.

DO YOU STILL BELIEVE IN LOVE? In spite of my generation's drive for money and status, we believe in love. And most of us believe that our lives will be judged more on the kind of person we were rather than what we were able to accumulate.

Service to humanity is our culture's highest calling. When all our days are done, the true measure of our lives will not be what we had or what we owned, but rather who we helped.

As a lasting thought, I have prepared an epitaph that I think could fit most of the wonderful people who live in the Lander Valley today and who almost all will be dead by the time you read this in 2090. Most of this is my own idea, although some of it has been borrowed from various poems, songs, sayings and comments by others. I think it is especially appropriate here:

An epitaph for a generation

May this world be a better place because we were here;
May people smile when they think of our names;
May the mention of this generation bring happy memories;
When people of good cheer gather, and our names are
mentioned, let there be smiles not frowns...

May our lives be measured not by how much we took, but by
how much we gave...
When we're gone, let our good works linger on...
To reflect on the example of our lives...
When people talk about us, let them say we did our best...

Instead of riches, let people say we were honest...
Instead of business success, let people say we were good
spouses, good parents, and good friends...
Instead of luck, let people say we worked hard...
We measured success by the people we helped and the friends we
made, not by the wealth accumulated...

Judge us by the kind of children we raised in this world;
And by the kind of work we accomplished
And the causes that we championed and the risks that we took;
For battles won and lost that had good intentions...

Let's hope when that final judgment is reached, it would be said
that we made the world a better place for our being here
these brief years:
That we were strong not mean; firm not stubborn; willing to try
new ideas and ways:
For we loved this valley so much...and love, like a smile, is
always returned back to the giver twicefold:
First, in affection communicated and second, in the warmth
reflected back.

ONE HUNDRED YEARS AGO IN WYOMING, back in 1890, there were
no cars, no airplanes, no computers or television sets. Paved roads
and telephones were very rare. The changes that have occurred in the
last 10 decades will pale compared to what our future residents will
be enjoying and enduring in the next ten decades.

Let's hope there will be no more wars in the next 100 years
although there seems to be always a threat of one somewhere in the
world.

Let's make a few predictions.

I foresee a world that is divided into nation states with China
looming as a major world power. This is quite different from today.

I see North America's standard of living rising and falling over the decades as our living styles clash with our abilities to do business.

We will have established space colonies by 2090, although I would predict they would not be as successful as space stations.

The problem of high speed travel will be solved, which will revolutionize how people get from one country to another and from outer space back to Earth. Time travel will be nearly a reality as speeds approach that of light.

On a more serene level, people will still enjoy feeding the trout at the Sinks. Arrowheads will be spotted in the Red Desert, although authorities will still be trying to keep people from picking them up. The Indian tribes will be fending off white people who want to have an Indian experience in 2090, just as they do today.

Wyoming will be mined in ways we can only imagine today as the state continues to provide valuable resources to the rest of the country.

And finally, a few more wild guesses:

- Yellowstone will have a major earthquake, which will ultimately make it even more popular with tourists. This will result in construction of some sort of monorail along the roadway to better transport tourists.
- Lander mayor Mark Keiser III will issue a special proclamation on the state's 200th birthday.
- And newspaper editor Michael Sniffin Jr. will write an editorial speculating on the future of the Lander Valley in the year 2190. And it won't be any more accurate than this one.

I WOULD LIKE TO CONCLUDE this message with an old Irish toast:

May the road rise up to meet you,
And the wind always be at your back
And let the sun shine brightly on your face
and the rains fall softly upon your fields

And until we meet again,
may God hold you in the palm of His hand.

Afterword

I love this place!

THIS BOOK IS FULL OF REFERENCES about how much I love Wyoming and Fremont County, in particular.

And I am not alone in this passion.

Let me tell you about just a few other people who have been maintaining a love affair with The Best Part Of America.

The Community Resource Coordinator for Lander, Linda Hewitt, is another passionate Lander lover. She is also a transplanted Iowan. "I love this place!" she often exclaims.

She was manager of the local chamber of commerce for many years and still can't help maintaining that type of go-go demeanor when it comes to community projects.

The completion of Lander's Main Street project just would not have happened without her. Lander has a new $4 million Main Street, courtesy of the citizens of the community and various state agencies.

And if you have a few hours (or days) sometime, she will tell you all the good things about living in this part of the country. Her phone number is (307) 332-2224. Her fax number is 332-4317.

Another big Lander booster is Paula McCormick, who is the Chamber manager. She came to Lander for the National Outdoor Leadership School and has been unrelenting in her efforts to improve the quality of life in our community.

Persons wanting information about The Best Part Of America can contact her at (307) 332-3892. The Chamber also has an out-of-state toll-free phone number of (800) 433-0662.

Fremont County, also known as Wind River Country, is ably represented by the Wind River Visitors Council. A capable woman, Liz Atchley, of Dubois, can give you all the information you want by calling her at (800) 645-6233.

WILLIAM CHARLES SNIFFIN, 47, is editor, publisher and, with his wife Nancy, owner of the *Lander Wyoming State Journal.* The *Journal* has a long tradition of prize-winning journalism, having won over 50 National Newspaper Association awards since Sniffin became editor in 1970. He has won three national and four state awards for his column writing.

Sniffin and his wife Nancy have 24 full- and part-time employees at the twice-weekly *Journal.* The paper is based in Lander, Wyoming, a small town located between the vast Red Desert and the towering Wind River Mountains in west-central Wyoming. The *Journal* has about 4,000 subscribers.

The *Journal* has been a trendsetter in recent years. It was the first newspaper in the Rocky Mountain Region to use desktop publishing, and it was the first newspaper in Wyoming printed on recycled paper. Since 1970, 14 *Journal* employees have gone on to become newspaper publishers.

Sniffin took time off in 1986 to earn a master's degree from the Centre for Journalism Studies at the University of Wales in Great Britain. He has since hosted five British interns who have worked at the *Journal.*

His master's thesis was titled *The Newspaper of the Future.* A portion of it, titled "The Era of the Editor," was published in ANPA's *presstime Magazine* in February, 1988.

Besides the *Journal*, the Sniffins also publish a weekly newspaper called the *Wind River News,* which serves the members of the neighboring Shoshone and Arapaho tribes and has a circulation of 2,000. They also own the *Winner Advocate,* a weekly in South Dakota, which is published by daughter and son-in-law Shelli and Jerry Johnson.

Sniffin has been active in both the Wyoming Press Association and the National Newspaper Association. He was one of the youngest presidents the WPA ever elected, heading that organization in 1980 at the age of 34. He has also presented a number of seminars at NNA conventions.

Sniffin is a past chairman of the Wyoming Travel Commission. He is a co-founder of Rocky Mountain International, a company that does European marketing for the states of Wyoming, Montana, Idaho, and South Dakota. The company has offices in Lander, Cheyenne, Laramie, London and Frankfurt.

Sniffin was born in Iowa and attended college there. He and his wife have four children.

For more information

PEOPLE WHO WANT to read Bill Sniffin's articles on a more regular basis can do so by subscribing to the twice-weekly *Wyoming State Journal.*

Subscription rates for one year are as follows:
Within Fremont County: $28.75
Outside of Fremont County: $33.75

Please mail your check to:
Wyoming State Journal
P.O. Box 900
Lander, Wyoming 82520

FOR ADDITIONAL COPIES of this book, check with your favorite local bookstore, or send your check for $12.95 to WCS Corporation, Publisher, at the address listed above.